A Woman's Way

The Stop-Smoking Book for Women

By Mary Embree

A Division of WRS Group, Inc.
Waco, Texas

Text © 1995 by Mary Embree

All rights reserved. No part of this book may be reproduced or transmitted in any form or by any means, electronic or mechanical, including photocopying or recording or by any information storage or retrieval system, without permission in writing from the publisher.

First published in the United States of America in 1995 by WRS Publishing, A division of WRS Group, Inc., 701 N. New Road, Waco, Texas 76710
Book design by Yvonne Chiu
Jacket design by Joe James

10 9 8 7 6 5 4 3 2 1
Library of Congress Cataloging-in-Publication Data

Embree, Mary
    A woman's way : the stop-smoking book for women / by Mary Embree.
       p. cm.
   ISBN 1-56796-081-2: $10.95
   1. Smoking cessation programs. 2. Women—Tobacco use. 3. Cigarette
habit—Treatment. 4. Self-help techniques. I. Title.
HV5746.E47   1995
613.85—dc20

                                                   94-43409
                                                     CIP

Dedication

*This book is dedicated to my mother,
Mary Elizabeth Nunn Cronkrite,
whom I miss very much.*

Table of Contents

Dedication v

Acknowledgments ix

Chapter 1   A Cigarette Is NOT a Woman's Friend 1

Chaper 2   Pregnancy, Premenstrual Syndrome and Menopause 21

Chapter 3   Quitting Gradually or "Cold Turkey" 43

Chapter 4   Remove the Blocks and Change Your Mind 53

Chapter 5   Get in Touch With Yourself 73

Chapter 6   Create Negative Associations With Smoking 87

Chapter 7   Replace Your Addiction With Something Better 99

Chapter 8   Deep Breathing, Relaxation and Visualization 109

Chapter 9   Exercise and the Nonsmoking Diet 125

Chapter 10   Putting It All Together— Ten Easy Steps 145

Chapter 11   Reinforce Your Resolve 155

Chapter 12   Now You're Really Living 165

Acknowledgments

I wish to acknowledge the encouragement I have received from the American Lung Association of Ventura County. Edna Ray, executive director, Barbara Weinberg, associate director, and all of the dedicated employees of the ALA have been enormously helpful and enthusiastically supportive of me from the first time I mentioned my plan to write this book to its completion. I want to give special thanks to G. H. "Jerry" Leavitt, associate director and master trainer, Freedom from Smoking Program of the American Lung Association, who has given me the benefit of his wealth of experience in smoking cessation programs and has been there for me every step of the way for advice and information. As they have stated that they believe this book has "broken new ground in the pursuit of ways to help women stop smoking," we plan to collaborate in presenting future programs aimed at girls and women, combining our expertise.

I would also like to thank gynecologist Allen L. Lawrence, M.D., Ph.D., and his wife, nutritionist Lisa Lawrence, M.S., Ph.D., for their professional advice on premenstrual syndrome, menopausal symptoms, and diet. Their book (which I edited), *A Doctor's Proven Nutritional Program for Conquering PMS*, published by Parker Publishing, served as a great resource of information on PMS and menopause, which I was able to draw upon in doing the research for my book.

Although they started out as clients, the Lawrences, whose books I continue to edit, have become very dear personal friends.

During the two years of research I did prior to writing *A Woman's Way*, I have received help from many sources. My book is based upon both public and private research, U.S. government reports, information from and the experience of several smoking cessation programs, interviews with medical doctors, psychotherapists, nutritionists, and smoking cessation facilitators, and various professionals involved in the field who have been generous in providing me with research data and their own perspectives.

Without the research and assistance of the many, many dedicated people who are seeking ways to reach smokers and encourage them to quit, this book could not have been written.

Chapter 1
A Cigarette Is NOT a Woman's Friend

Smoking is not the same addiction in women as it is in men. Men and women start smoking, continue smoking and quit smoking for very different reasons. By the mid-1990s female smokers will outnumber males. By the year 2000, the death rate of women from smoking will surpass the men's death rate.

And yet there are few, if any, major stop-smoking programs dealing with the issues of women's addiction to nicotine. Mixing women and men in the same smoking-cessation program is not as beneficial to women as a program for women only would be.

There are several reasons for this. A woman's menstrual cycle has a great deal to do with the way she smokes and her ability to quit, and therefore is a factor which must be addressed. Women are reluctant to discuss these personal matters in the presence of men. Another reason that a smoking cessation program should not be mixed is the fact that men find it easier to quit than women do. This can be very demoralizing to women.

This book addresses these differences. It shows you, a girl or a woman who is finding it hard to quit smoking, how to break your addiction without the usual pain associated with quitting and without gaining weight. At the same time, it tells you how you can learn to build your self-confidence, gain self-esteem and take control of your life.

What are the particular risks to females and how are they different from the risks to males? The following facts have been taken from recent reports from the New England Journal of Medicine, various publications of the U.S. Department of Health and Human Services and a number of scientific studies:

- Women are three times more likely to get lung cancer from smoking than men. Among women, lung cancer now causes more deaths than breast cancer.

- The health effects for female smokers include increased risk of lung cancer, heart disease, kidney cancer, cervical neoplasia, invasive cervical cancer, endometrial cancer, earlier menopause, reduced fertility, increased spontaneous abortion rate and long-term and short-term adverse effects on fetuses, infants and children.

- Pregnant women who smoke have higher rates of miscarriages, stillbirths and premature births and experience more complications of pregnancy than nonsmokers.

- Newborns of smoking mothers are more likely to suffer crib death than babies of nonsmokers.

- Children of smoking mothers suffer a higher rate of lung diseases such as asthma, bronchitis and pneumonia than children of nonsmoking parents.

- Menstrual cramps, premenstrual syndrome and menopausal symptoms are worsened by smoking.

- Myocardial infarction (heart attack) in women smoking 35 or more cigarettes a day is 20 times higher than among nonsmokers.

- The risk of stroke for a woman smoker who uses oral contraceptives or estrogen replacement therapy is profoundly increased. For women 27 to 37 who smoke and take contraceptives, the risk is one per 8,400. For women 44 to 45 it is one per 250.

- The health effects appear to be much more severe in female smokers than in male smokers.

- After stopping smoking, a woman's risk of developing lung and laryngeal cancer drops slowly, equaling that of nonsmokers only after 10 to 15 years.

Here are some additional facts about smoking that *everyone* who smokes should be aware of:

- Each year more than 430,000 Americans die from the effects of smoking—more than all who died in World War II.

- As addictive as heroin and cocaine, nicotine from a puff of cigarette smoke reaches the brain in just seven seconds. That's twice as fast as heroin injected into a vein.

- It has been found that heavy smokers have a higher incidence of chromosomal aberrations. One of the reasons that smokers suffer more illnesses than nonsmokers is that smoking causes changes in the immune function. Smokers with malignant melanoma are more likely to develop metastases than nonsmokers.

According to a recent report from the Surgeon General titled, "The Health Consequences of Smoking—The Changing Cigarette," a new and major concern now is additives in cigarettes, the flavorings and chemicals which are added to enhance consumer acceptability. The carcinogenic effects of these added substances are not evaluated. Information on additives is not available to the Public Health Service because, in fact, *manufacturers are not even required to provide this information.*

No agency of the federal government exercises oversight or regulatory authority in the manufacture of cigarettes. This, however, may be changing. In early 1994, Commissioner David A. Kessler of the Food and Drug Administration concluded that the FDA could regulate cigarettes as it does drugs because nicotine is highly addictive. Walker Merryman of the Tobacco Institute declared, "No one should underestimate the ability or willingness of this industry to very vigorously defend itself."

There are several thousand constituents identified

in tobacco and tobacco smoke with nicotine being the worst. Even if a smoker were to shift to a less hazardous cigarette, doing so may actually increase the hazard because in most cases, smokers simply smoke more cigarettes or inhale deeper. No matter what or how a person smokes, there is *no such thing as a safe cigarette*.

There is also a monetary price that we all pay for this addiction. Smoking accounts for **$65 billion** per year in health-care costs and loss of productivity. We all pay for smoking.

These are the horrifying facts about smoking. These are facts that both women and men must know in order to be able to see smoking in its true light. But scaring smokers isn't enough to make them quit for good. That only works for awhile. And this book isn't only about living longer, it is also about living a better, healthier and happier life and about protecting fetuses and children from the deleterious effects of smoking.

My mother died of heart disease. The tragedy isn't just that smoking cut short her life, it greatly affected the quality of her life. She was ill much of the time with diseases often associated with smoking—bronchitis, pneumonia, emphysema, allergies, chronic fatigue and heart palpitations. I can't recall a time when she didn't cough. From her early twenties she had smoked one to two packs of cigarettes a day. My mother was second from the youngest. Three of her four sisters were older than she. They are all still healthy and one of them turns 90 this year. None of them smokes.

Over and over again Mom had been told to quit, but she said she just enjoyed it too much to give up. No one could convince her that good health would be more enjoyable. My mother was intelligent, kind and loving and I miss her very much. This book is for her.

It's also for my niece, Lisa, who died of smoke inhalation. She had gone to sleep with a cigarette in her hand. It fell between the cushions of the couch she was lying on and smoldered for an hour or so before the couch burst into flame. Lisa suffered third-degree burns over 30 percent of her body, but it was the smoke that killed her. She lingered in a coma for three weeks before dying. She was 25 years old when her life was snuffed out.

We must quit only for ourselves

Even though women's smoking often affects their children as well, ultimately, they must quit smoking primarily for themselves. If they do it for someone else, it is likely that they will return to smoking because they will resent being deprived of something they "enjoyed."

The very fact that you are reading this book means that you have taken the first step toward quitting— and that first step is crucial. Because the most important element in quitting smoking is admitting that you really need to. The next step may be a bit harder—*wanting* to quit.

There are many books on stopping smoking and many programs using different approaches. And some of them seem to work for some people. It may well be that if you are truly ready and do most of what is suggested, any of these books or programs will help you. During my extensive research over the years, however, I have not yet found a program that has been designed specifically for women who smoke. As in most of medical research, most of the studies have been done on men, though studies have shown that it is harder for women to quit smoking than it is for men.

In most of the programs that are available, the process is painful and the presenters, or facilitators, of the programs stress the negatives: how "bad" it is for you, how much you are going to have to "work" at it and how "hard" it is going to be to quit.

They also warn you that once you've quit, even one puff will hook you again: "You're only a puff away from a pack a day," is a favorite saying in one of the programs. While this may be true in some cases, it certainly is not true for everyone. In fact, studies show that, for many people, the more often they quit, the fewer cigarettes they smoke when they do start up again. Although it's good to be on guard, taking one puff is not a guarantee that you will resume smoking a pack a day. Without realizing it, telling a woman this could set it up for her to do just that.

What you are going to find here is quite different. You know the health consequences of smoking. These were clearly outlined at the beginning of the book. And, let's face it, you'd have to have been living on another planet not to know that smoking is bad for you. But even though you know that, it hasn't been enough to make you give it up.

You haven't quit yet because you don't want to give up *something you love*, you don't want to say goodbye forever to *an old friend* (the cigarette), you don't want to *gain weight* and you don't want to feel *deprived*. You just want to reach a point where you no longer crave that nicotine fix. Because you know even as you are holding that cigarette that it's the cigarette that is really holding you.

You also know that smoking isn't considered very attractive anymore. It certainly is not feminine or sexy. You never hear of people who want a cigarette *before sex*. If you smoke, in fact, it will very likely decrease your sex drive. Not only can it take longer for a man to get and maintain an erection, but smoking has been linked to impotence. One recent study found that men who smoke are *two and a half times as likely* to become impotent in their thirties. For a woman, it may reduce her libido and interfere with her ability to have an orgasm. As a vasoconstrictor, it can have a numbing effect on a lot of things.

When you started smoking it was probably acceptable almost anywhere. Certainly, there wasn't the stigma attached to it that there was to other addictions, such as heavy drinking. You probably didn't even know then that nicotine is probably the strongest addictive drug known to mankind. It is also quite possibly the most damaging physically. More people die of it than from *all other drugs combined.*

I have known some talented and intelligent jazz and rock musicians who were addicted to cocaine or heroin in their younger years and kicked it. I've known many former alcoholics who have been clean for years. Yet, among both of these groups, many are still smoking cigarettes. They'll readily admit that smoking is the one addiction that they have been unable to conquer. If you've had a tough time coming to terms with your addiction to cigarettes, you are not alone.

Now, since the Surgeon General has linked secondhand smoke with illness, including lung cancer in nonsmokers, and the Environmental Protection Agency has identified it as a first-class carcinogen, it's hard to find a place where you can indulge your addiction. You can't smoke on a plane, a bus, in many airports, in more and more restaurants, in friends' homes or even outdoors in many public places. As a smoker you have become a social pariah to a large segment of the population.

And, getting back to it's *not* being sexy, most of the nonsmoking men and women I know won't date a smoker because they don't like the way they smell. They wouldn't consider kissing them any more than they would consider licking a dirty ashtray. And what about marriage and a family? It isn't just a smoking mother whose addiction can harm a developing fetus. Twice as many babies are born with deformities if their *father* is a smoker even if their mother does not smoke.

You're aware of all the biases against people who smoke and you'd probably really like to quit, but you've tried to before and it was so *painful*. You might also have gained weight—many women do.

Why do women smoke?

Why do women start smoking? Why do they continue and why do they find it so hard to quit?

- Most females started when they were teenagers.
- The average age for girls to start smoking is now 13.
- Girls start smoking as an act of rebellion.
- Girls and women continue to smoke to stay slim.
- Women smoke to relieve stress, loneliness or depression.
- There are now more teenage girls than boys who smoke. (More males have quit smoking than females.)

In recent years tobacco companies have been targeting women more and more as potential users of their products. The number of female smokers 12 to 18 years old doubled between 1977 and 1987 as a result of highly successful cigarette ad campaigns.

Fear of gaining weight

The fear of weight gain is the number one reason most women don't want to quit smoking. They believe that gaining weight is inevitable and surveys indicate that there is usually a five-pound weight gain, on average. There are many reasons for this. Among them is the fact that women oftentimes replace the urge for a cigarette with chocolate or other sweets. With a proper diet, the cravings for sweets aren't so intense. But more about this in a later chapter.

Unfortunately, modern American women equate thinness with beauty. They also feel that they can better control their weight by smoking cigarettes. It's no surprise that most of us think this way. We have been bombarded with this message for years. Through powerful advertising by cigarette, clothing and cosmetic manufacturers, girls and women have been told that to be truly desirable they must be thin, beautiful and independent. The Virginia Slims ad campaign is the quintessential example of this. They correlate smoking with independence: "You've come a long way, baby." Even the term "baby" implies youthful appeal, another bit of subliminal propaganda.

Self-image is everything to girls and young women who want to be popular and "with it." The cigarette ads show young, thin, attractive women having fun with great-looking men. Is it any wonder that most women who smoke started in their teens when they were the most impressionable? And the age at which girls start smoking is getting younger all the time. Currently, the average age of new smokers is 13.

Addictions started this young are incredibly hard to break. The teenage years are a difficult period for most people. If a teenage girl learns to handle her stress by smoking, she may never learn more positive, productive ways to deal with problems in her life. When stressful situations occur in later years, she will first think of a cigarette.

According to a survey recently conducted of women who were members of a professional women's network, the major reason they smoked was stress.

Most haven't quit because they haven't been able to. But there are a lot of women who simply don't want to quit, and the main reason they gave was fear of gaining weight. There were a number of them who, like my mother, didn't want to quit because they "enjoyed" it too much. It's hard for these women to understand that they don't really enjoy smoking. It's really that they are satisfying an urgent craving, much as any addict would be doing, whether she is addicted to alcohol, heroin or cocaine. After all, what's to enjoy about drawing hot, toxic smoke into your lungs?

Smoking and eating disorders

The more I've studied women's smoking addiction, the more I have seen the resemblance of this disorder to eating disorders. Girls and young women become anorexic and bulimic for the same reasons they smoke: as an act of rebellion. In each case the women experience a sense of independence. They have taken control of the one thing that is within their power to control: their bodies. The fact that these syndromes are self-destructive either doesn't occur to them or, if it does, it doesn't matter. In eating disorders as well as in smoking the goal is the same: to be thin. Thin is in. Many girls and women want to be thin even if it kills them. In the case of anorexia and smoking, it often does. The major difference in the pathology is that smoking usually takes longer to kill.

Interestingly, a large number of girls who smoke cigarettes do *not* drink, smoke marijuana or become sexually active, according to a 1992 survey by the Texas

Commission on Alcohol and Drug Abuse. They are concerned about the risks of using hard drugs, drinking alcohol and contracting sexually related diseases. They can see the immediate results of drug overdoses, automobile accidents and AIDS. But they don't worry about the potential cancers and cardiovascular diseases caused by smoking. The damaging effects of smoking are too far into the future. What happens to them when they turn 50 or 60 is of no concern—that's "old," anyway.

Most teenagers live for the moment and rarely think of the long-term consequences of their actions. Even when they are told that smoking causes premature wrinkling, they aren't worried. What matters is right now, today, and they want to be thin.

It isn't only teenage girls, however, who smoke to keep their weight down; it is the reason most women of any age give for not quitting. Weight gain isn't inevitable, though, when you quit smoking. Neither is suffering painful withdrawal symptoms.

You don't have to gain weight

The good news is that you may not find it painful to quit if you follow the suggestions in this book. In fact, quite soon you will probably feel better both physically and psychologically than you have in a very long time. As you become healthier physically and emotionally, you will find withdrawal from nicotine much easier than you expected it to be. And, as for gaining weight, well, you simply don't have to. You can eat as much as you did before, only differently, and not gain an ounce. If you add exercise into the mix, you have an even better chance at keeping your weight the same. Your attitude will have a lot to do with it, too. I've known women who actually lost weight when they quit smoking.

I once smoked. If I hadn't, I don't believe that I'd be qualified to write this book. Having worked as a therapist/facilitator with Schick Laboratories and the American Lung Association, I gratefully acknowledge the training and information I received from them. But their programs were not gender-specific and I believe there are easier and more effective ways of helping women stop smoking.

I started smoking when I was 16 because it was *cool*. My friends in high school smoked between classes, sneaking down the street in tight little groups to a corner away from the school where the teachers couldn't see them. To be "one of the gang" I learned to smoke, too. It wasn't easy at first. It made me cough, made my throat sore and tasted awful. But I finally mastered it, believing that it made me look sophisticated and more attractive to the group I wanted to impress. According to the California Department of Education, the single best predictor of whether a young person will smoke is whether she has a best friend who does. Peer pressure is powerful.

You, too, probably started in your teens. Almost everyone did. In fact, sixty percent of all those who currently smoke began by age 14. Ninety-five percent of smokers started before the age of 20. Those who started later generally smoke fewer cigarettes and find it easier to quit. *Addictions started young are much harder to break.*

You learned while you were still very impressionable to handle stress by smoking a cigarette. When you got nervous about something, you lit up. Now you will have to learn to handle stress in a whole different, and much healthier, way.

The hard way to quit

Many people quit smoking. Many people quit smoking many times. Those who *keep* quitting—because they keep starting up again—are those who do it the hard way. When you do it through sheer willpower you are doing it the hard way. You think of a cigarette all the time. You stand downwind of a smoker just to get a waft of their smoke. It still smells good to you. You feel deprived. You feel like you have given up a good friend. After all, that cigarette has been there for you every time you felt stressed, depressed, angry or lonely. It also partied with you. You smoked when you had a drink, when you had a cup of coffee, when you were relaxing, when you needed something to do with your hands at a party where you didn't know anyone. The ring of the telephone was a signal to light up. Smoking gave you something to do on your work breaks. You never had to be alone because it was always there.

I've heard women say, when they were planning to quit smoking, that they got frightened. They were afraid to quit and be out there on their own without that "friend" which was always there in times of need. They were also afraid that even if they were able to quit, they'd only go back to smoking again and would then feel like a failure.

Perhaps the saddest are those who say that they enjoy smoking. For them, giving it up is more than simply giving up a friend, it is giving up something which they believe makes them "happy" and some of these women are lonely and have very little happiness in their lives.

When people quit through sheer willpower, they feel they've lost something. They mourn. It feels like the end of a love affair. Something is missing in their lives. And their desire to have it back never completely goes away. This is the hard way.

Smoking and Self-Esteem

How often have you seen people who take drugs, get into fights, are always in trouble with the law, who drink too much or can't hold onto a job? When you see someone like that, you usually think, She's her own worst enemy. Anytime you do something that is self-destructive you are being your own enemy. When you know the hazards of smoking, you must realize that to continue doing it must be self-destructive.

Learn to love yourself

So the first thing you must do to overcome this addiction is to learn to love yourself. No matter how much anyone else loves you they can't break the addiction for you. They can't live your life for you and they can't die for you. In the end, all of us experience only ourselves. Since you're all you've got and your life is the only life you've got to live, it's time you started loving yourself with all your heart, mind and body. When you love yourself, you want to take care of yourself, and when you take care of yourself, life is more beautiful.

Everything that goes on in our lives, everyone we meet, everything we see, hear, smell, taste and feel is colored by our perception of it. What is beautiful to one person may be ugly to another. For instance, some people like the smell of a newly fertilized field because they think of new growth and abundant harvests. Other people only smell horse manure.

No matter what mistakes you have made or what addictions you may have it is important for you to see the beauty that is inside you. Any negative self-image you may have was probably put there by someone else and probably when you were very young. There may have been patterns in your life that created a need to smoke. But that doesn't mean that you are a helpless victim of your past. You are responsible for yourself now. There is no reason why someone else's opinion should influence your opinion of yourself. That is only his or her perception. What is your perception of yourself? Whatever it is now and in the future is up to you. Your life, your health and your happiness are your responsibility. They are in your hands. You have the power to change your life.

The classic definition of the difference between the optimist and the pessimist is whether she/he sees the cup as half-full or as half-empty. If we are unhappy with ourselves, we will see ourselves like a cup that is half-empty. The more unhappy we are, the more empty we feel. We want to fill this void and, too often, end up filling it with quick fixes and momentary pleasures. But next morning those pleasures may have turned into headaches, and we end up having drained that half-empty cup even more.

We must learn to be our own best friend

Because it is still a world governed primarily by men, women often have problems with self-esteem. To break this chain we must start seeing ourselves as lovable; we must become our own best friend. When we have a best friend, we always want to be there for her when she needs us. We care about her and treat her with kindness. We don't want anyone or anything to hurt her. We want her to have a long, happy, prosperous and healthy life. When we are our own best friend, we want all of these things for ourselves.

Any time you allow something to abuse your body or your mind, you are not being your own best friend. Cigarettes take you hostage; they use you and abuse you. They try to trick you into thinking that they are good for you. They are there for you when you are lonely, nervous or angry. They give you temporary consolation and instant gratification. They make you like them, want them, even need them. They party with you and convince you that you're having a good time while they are surreptitiously doing their dirty work, ravaging your lungs, vandalizing your vital organs, poisoning your body and robbing you of your youth and vitality. They entice you into spending a lot of time with them. They give you a little pleasure and fleeting comfort, and then, when you least suspect it, they take over your mind, causing you to believe things like, "I really enjoy smoking," or "I don't think they are doing me any harm," or "I can quit anytime I want to." They may be seductive and fun to be with, but they are not your friend. Cigarettes are your enemy.

Chapter 2

Pregnancy, Premenstrual Syndrome and Menopause

Smoking during pregnancy

As most women know by now, pregnancy and smoking should never go together. The *1969 U.S. Public Health Service Report* confirmed the association between maternal smoking and low-birth-weight babies, an increased incidence of prematurity, spontaneous abortions, stillbirths and neonatal deaths. The 1971 report concluded that maternal smoking during pregnancy exerts a retarding influence on fetal growth. In 1973, cigarette smoking was found to be a probable cause of increased late fetal mortality and infant mortality. Impaired intellectual development of the offspring was associated with smoking during pregnancy in 1978.

A pregnant woman literally smokes for two. When she smokes, the chemicals taken into her body flow through the placenta to her unborn child. In a study involving 53,000 smokers conducted by the Pennsylvania State University College of Medicine, their babies ran a 50 percent higher risk of developing Sudden Infant Death Syndrome. According to a British study, children of smokers lag three to five months behind others in reading and math. Study after study has indicated that there is three times the rate of birth defects in babies born to smoking mothers.

If you are pregnant or planning to become pregnant, quitting smoking is imperative. It could be the difference between life and death for your baby. The National Center for Health Statistics has estimated that if all pregnant women stopped smoking, the number of fetal and infant deaths would be reduced by approximately 10 percent.

Smoking and oral contraceptives

If you are smoking and taking birth control pills, your risk of stroke is incredibly high. Even for those women who are not taking birth control pills, the risk of stroke is high. Women smoking one to fourteen cigarettes a day have a relative risk of fatal and nonfatal stroke of 2.2 compared with nonsmoking women. Those who smoke 25 or more per day have a 3.7 relative risk of stroke. Add to this mix birth control pills and you might as well be playing Russian roulette. The good news is that when women stop smoking, there is a prompt decrease in stroke risk.

The connection between premenstrual tension and smoking

As smokers jokingly say, quitting was easy for me. I'd done it dozens of times. In every case, I started again in about three weeks. I always knew that if I could get past that three-week mark, I'd be home free. And it was true. Once I got past that particular period, I had quit for good.

Chapter 2

I never made any connection between that three-week time frame and my menstrual cycle until recently when I edited a book called *A Doctor's Proven Nutritional Program for Conquering PMS* by Allen Lawrence, M.D., and Lisa Lawrence, M.S. (Parker Publishing Company). Like a light bulb switching on over my head I realized that the reason I had always started smoking again after three weeks was because of the premenstrual syndrome.

From about three days to a week before my period was to start I'd get depressed, irritable and nervous. Even though I'd had the emotional strength to keep from smoking up to then, my emotions would overwhelm me and I'd light up again. After three weeks, nicotine has almost completely left your system, so it wasn't a physical addiction I was experiencing. It was a psychological addiction. I wanted something that would make me feel better and I associated a cigarette with relief of stress.

At that time, I wasn't aware that I was suffering from PMS (although my family suggested I might be). I thought it was the normal ups and downs everyone experiences in their lives. Even if I had suspected it, I doubt that I would have thought that anything could be done about it.

Now we realize that a lot can be done about premenstrual syndrome with diet and/or hormone therapy. We women don't have to suffer as we once did. If PMS is a problem for you, this might very well be the reason that you have found it so hard to quit smoking. I am certain now that it played a large role in the difficulties I faced.

Like a vicious cycle, PMS makes it harder for a

woman to quit smoking—and smoking makes her PMS worse. It would seem, as my mother used to say, that you can't win for losing. Another way of looking at it, however, is that this interconnection gives you the opportunity to heal both problems. You just may find that by conquering your PMS, the next challenge, quitting smoking, may be a much easier step than you could have imagined.

Male Cycles

As women's cycles are clearly influenced by hormones, is there a hormonally controlled biological rhythm with men, too? Probably, but it is much less obvious. In cases where the male hormone, testosterone, is excessive or is absent, there are definite personality changes. Men with more than one Y chromosome are often very aggressive or even violent. Men whose testosterone production has been stopped become docile and calm. It was castrated men, eunuchs, who watched over harems centuries ago because they were gentle with women and had no sex drive.

Even though men do not have fluctuations in their hormones monthly as women do, they have reported feeling cyclic changes. Dr. Daniel J. Levinson of Yale University School of Medicine found that a man's life can be divided into four phases, or "seasons." A man usually experiences a "mid-life transition" between the ages of 40 and 45. It is a crisis time for many of them, and they may become irrational and be regarded as "upset" or "sick." Men have also reported being affected by outside forces such as phases of the moon or weather conditions. There is an old myth that the moon makes men insane and sex-craved. Crime statistics would seem to bear this out. In any event, 90 percent of violent crimes are committed by men. And, although women may attempt suicide more often, more men actually succeed in taking their own lives.

When men and women both realize that there are certain times in their lives, whether it's once a month, once a year or four times in a lifetime, when they need an extra amount of understanding and tenderness, their relationships will drastically improve.

The Menstrual Cycle

Female babies are born with two ovaries, each of which contain thousands of egg cells. In response to a message from the pituitary gland, one of the unripe egg cells develops within a ring of cells which gradually forms a balloon or cyst called the Graafian follicle. These cells make the hormone estrogen. The egg cell, when it is fully developed, appears as a blister on the surface of the ovary. Then, at a message from the pituitary gland, it bursts and releases the mature egg cell in a process known as ovulation.

In a journey that takes several days, the egg cell makes its way down the fallopian tubes to the womb. The scar tissue that is left behind becomes the *corpus luteum*, which produces the pregnancy hormone, progesterone. The progesterone relaxes the uterus and turns its lining into a soft, spongy nest in which the fertilized egg can implant itself. If a pregnancy occurs, estrogen and progesterone levels stay high. If not, that soft, spongy lining disintegrates and is shed, progesterone and estrogen levels drop rapidly, and menstruation is triggered. One menstrual cycle ends and another begins.

There are considerable variations in women's menstrual cycles. Menstrual flow may be pink and watery or thick and red. Menstruation may occur anywhere between every 21 days to every 36 days and last from 3 to 7 days. All of these variations are considered normal and compatible with full reproductive functioning.

Estrogen and progesterone first peak and then fall during the last half of the menstrual cycle, the 14 days between ovulation and menstruation. It is when these two surging hormones lose their balance that premenstrual syndrome appears.

What are the symptoms of premenstrual syndrome?

How do you know if you have premenstrual syndrome? There are many symptoms, both physical and psychological, and they occur in the week or two before the start of your period. They can last for as briefly as one day or for as long as two weeks. Among them are:

Swelling of the hands, feet or ankles
Painful swelling of the breasts
Abdominal bloating
Weight gain
Stomachache
Headache
Backache

Aching joints
Insomnia
Fatigue
Unexplainable sadness
Depression
Lethargy
Crying for no apparent reason
Irritability, angry outbursts
Anxiety, mood swings
Suicidal thoughts
Cravings for sweets, especially for chocolate
Acne
Asthma
Hay fever

Most women have experienced some of these symptoms during the week or two before her period. According to the Lawrences, more than 150 different symptoms have now been attributed to PMS. These symptoms involve almost every organ in the body and range from mild mood swings to suicidal feelings, from a general sense of malaise to excruciating migraine headache.

During this time of the month, women often have uncontrollable food binges. Not only do they eat too much, they usually eat the wrong things, which exacerbates their PMS symptoms and causes weight gain. Feeling stressed, they may have an alcoholic drink to calm them down. Alcohol acts like sugar and the body metabolizes it so rapidly that within a short while they need another drink, then another to maintain the sense of relaxation. Inadvertently, through this mechanism, they risk becoming alcoholics.

If they are smokers they'll smoke more than usual in this premenstrual time period to try to get relief. Even if they have been successful in keeping from smoking for two or three weeks prior to that time, the feelings of anxiety and depression become overwhelming and they give in to the urge to smoke. And, as alcohol and nicotine are drugs, they only make the symptoms worse in the long run.

Many women with PMS suffer from medical conditions such as allergies, boils, herpes, hives, asthma, sinus infections, bladder infections, laryngitis, abdominal pain or even epileptic seizures.

Even if your symptoms are not as severe as the ones mentioned above, they may be serious enough to make your attempts at quitting smoking difficult or even impossible. According to a 1988 report by the U.S. Department of Health and Human Services, stress has been shown to affect the initiation of smoking and the smoking rate, as well as relapse following smoking cessation. It appears to be a factor especially in influencing women's ability to stop smoking as well as in their starting smoking.

Join a support group

Research into the role of social support in buffering stress suggests that women's efforts to stop smoking may benefit from interpersonal support more than those of men. This is an important reason to join a stop-smoking program, especially if you can find one that is geared specifically for women, or to find a friend and form a "buddy system."

Joining a support group of women suffering from PMS or women going through menopause could also be very beneficial. By reducing your stress, you will find it easier to stop smoking and remain a nonsmoker.

What causes PMS?

What is PMS and what causes it? PMS is caused by an imbalance of two female hormones, estrogen and progesterone. A PMS woman seems to have higher estrogen levels in relation to progesterone. In the week or two prior to her menstrual period, estrogen is at its highest. If her diet does not contain sufficient amounts of vitamin B_6 or magnesium, her liver cannot break down estrogen. That's when PMS symptoms develop. The Lawrences, as well as many other researchers, believe that PMS is a nutritional-deficiency syndrome that creates the imbalance between estrogen and progesterone.

It is also believed that the fluctuation of estrogen and progesterone may be initially orchestrated by brain hormones which influence and are influenced by a woman's response to her personal environment. Such external forces as stress, sadness, travel, weight-gain or -loss, divorce, surgery, job changes, moving or other traumatic events may influence the neuroendocrine system and, in turn, the menstrual cycle. The brain's neuroendocrine mechanisms may also be responsible for irregular menstrual flow or loss of menstruation. In fact, there is such a close interaction between the brain and the menstrual pattern that a group of women living together in a college dorm might find their menstrual cycles synchronized.

A woman's lifestyle and medical history contribute to the intensity of her PMS. When she understands how her PMS relates to certain influences, she may be able to alter the way she lives her life. Premenstrual syndrome has been shown clearly to be a mind/body condition that encompasses physical and psychological symptoms.

If you have severe PMS, you should see your doctor and get a complete physical examination. Even if you have mild symptoms that are typical of PMS, some of which are listed above, these can be symptoms of something else and a potentially more serious condition. Although changing your diet may alleviate your symptoms, you might be a candidate for hormone therapy as well. These are important issues you should talk over with your physician.

There are a number of medical approaches to PMS. Some are appropriate and some are not. If your doctor suggests that you have a hysterectomy, a D&C or get pregnant to cure your symptoms, you should immediately seek another doctor. As it is the result of a hormonal imbalance, PMS cannot be treated by surgery. Often PMS symptoms worsen after surgery or pregnancy. You should also beware of any physician who prescribes tranquilizers or antidepressants as these only mask the condition, may delay proper treatment and can cause even greater problems.

For many women, their PMS symptoms

intensified when they were on tranquilizers and their depressions only deepened. A mild tranquilizer, taken for a limited time may help you get through an extremely anxious time in your life, but it should only be taken when nothing else works.

Antidepressants have to build in potency within the body, and it may take weeks or even months before a woman feels any effect from them. As PMS is cyclic, antidepressants are not a logical choice of treatment. A more natural approach would be to take the B vitamins.

With each pregnancy, the likelihood of getting PMS increases. That may be because the need for B vitamins and magnesium, along with the need for other vitamins and minerals increases. If a woman's diet was depleted before pregnancy, she will very likely be even more depleted after pregnancy.

While a woman often develops PMS in her early twenties, it usually worsens with age. By age 35, she may be so troubled with symptoms that she will need to seek help.

There is evidence that PMS may run in families. You may have a greater predisposition to it because of a gene passed from mother to daughter.

The PMS diet

How and what you eat play a very big part in maintaining a normal hormone balance. By adjusting your diet during your cycle, you can avoid the disturbing mood swings that make it so much harder to remain a nonsmoker.

Just before their period women are often overtaken by cravings for certain foods. It may be salt, sugar or starch, and they give in to them, actually making their PMS worse. As the female hormone estrogen binds with salt, a craving for salty potato chips or pretzels could indicate that they have an overabundance of estrogen. Yet estrogen causes the body to store salt and salt retains body fluids. They therefore will see their abdomen, hands and feet swell from fluid retention. Even more serious effects of giving in to a salt craving are migraine-like headaches and tension. Not only a woman's hands and feet but her brain swells, too. The swelling stretches the surrounding brain membrane, which can't expand beyond the skull, thus irritating the membrane's sensitive nerves. This can cause not only headaches but dizziness, sensitivity to light, agitation and a general tension.

Women with these symptoms must reduce their salt intake and drink a lot of fluids to help cleanse their bodies and flush out waste products.

Those who crave carbohydrates, especially sweets, may have PMS symptoms which are similar to hypoglycemia. A half-hour to an hour after she consumes a donut, candy bar or other sugary snack she may experience a fainting spell, heart palpitations, fatigue or a headache. In the last half of the menstrual cycle, cells bind insulin and a high insulin level makes the body's blood sugar drop rapidly. Eating sweets stimulates insulin production and then insulin makes the blood sugar level drop.

Chapter 2

The best way to avoid these cravings is to eat small amounts of food every three or four hours. This will prevent the blood sugar from dropping to the point of intense sugar cravings.

Although it is always important to eat a balanced, nutritious diet, eating the right foods is of the utmost importance during the PMS phase of your cycle. The "right foods" are those which have more magnesium than calcium in them. These are whole grains, cereals, beans, fresh vegetables and fresh fruits. It is best to eat foods that have at least a 2 to 1 ratio of magnesium to calcium. And, of course, the fresher, the better. Some of these are:

- bananas
- coconut milk
- avocados
- beets
- green peas
- black beans
- corn
- wheat germ
- brown rice
- sesame seeds
- rice bran
- whole grain pasta
- cashews
- peanuts & peanut butter
- acorns
- passion fruit
- mushrooms
- potatoes
- black-eyed peas
- lima beans
- bell pepper
- corn meal
- oatmeal
- oat bran
- whole grain barley
- buckwheat
- pine nuts
- pumpkin seeds
- chestnuts
- walnuts

During the PMS phase of your cycle it's best to avoid dairy products, alcohol, caffeine, processed foods and foods high in calcium. The major foods to avoid during this period are:

milk	cream cheese
yogurt	caffeinated coffee
chocolate	alcoholic drinks
candy	apples
desserts with sugar	ice cream
mangoes	guavas
carrots	pineapples
peaches	cabbage
kale	mustard greens
watercress	lettuce
olives	broccoli
cauliflower	sweet potatoes
asparagus	spinach
Brussels sprouts	white bread
French bread	pita bread (white)

All of the foods in both lists (with the possible exception of breads made with enriched white flour) are okay to eat during the rest of the month. The more natural, unprocessed foods are better for you than processed foods and most fast foods. They are also less likely to cause weight gain.

The importance of limiting or eliminating alcohol consumption

When you are trying to quit smoking, it is always imperative to limit your consumption of alcohol. This is not only because it worsens PMS symptoms but because it lowers your resistance to temptation.

Before I quit smoking I would often have a martini before dinner. At a party, I would have a couple of highballs. I discovered, to my dismay, that I always craved a cigarette with a drink—more then than at any other time. One night at a party, just after I had quit smoking, I found myself lifting the glass to my lips whenever I really wanted to take a puff from a cigarette. Within a short time, I had had too much to drink, and that night when I got home I became very ill.

Since I associated wine with dinner and never with a cigarette, I stopped drinking hard liquor entirely and switched to wine. I found that I cut down on my drinking considerably and, after awhile, never had a desire to drink hard liquor again. I'm sure this was a healthy choice.

If you don't drink, this will not be a problem for you. But, if you do, I strongly suggest that you abstain for the first few weeks after you quit smoking. If you don't wish to do that, then switch to something you do not associate with smoking and drink even that very sparingly.

Whenever you are feeling blue or depressed it is best not to drink at all. Alcohol is a depressant and only makes your depression worse. Maybe not at the time you are actually drinking, but later, when the effects wear off. The same is true for sweets. They elevate your blood sugar and then, when the blood sugar level drops, it goes below normal and creates a depression. Sudden mood swings are often associated with sugar intake.

Women with PMS also have a decreased alcohol tolerance. Some women actually find that even one glass of wine makes them feel a little intoxicated when they drink it during their premenstrual period. A survey which appeared in the Archives of General Psychiatry indicated that 67 percent of menstruating female alcoholics linked their drinking patterns to their cycles. *All of the women questioned stated that their drinking problems either started or became worse during their premenstrual days.*

It is important not to drink on an empty stomach. Whenever you do drink you should eat small protein snacks such as nuts, chicken wings, cheese, or hors d'oeuvres made with fish or meat since food tempers the effects of alcohol.

Smoking and menopause

Women who smoke enter menopause earlier than women who don't. It is possible that the early age of menopause among smokers may contribute to the risk of osteoporosis. Women begin to lose bone after the age of thirty-five at the rate of about one percent a year. At fifty, bone mass loss accelerates to about one and a half percent for the next ten years, then levels off again to one percent a year. The Western beauty ideal contributes to the risk of osteoporosis. Women at major risk are fair-skinned, thin, smokers and those who have had an early menopause.

Again, and it can't be emphasized enough, smoking causes an earlier menopause and creates a greater risk of osteoporosis. In addition to quitting smoking, the best results in treating this condition are obtained through exercise, magnesium and calcium supplements and estrogen.

The aging effects of smoking have been clearly documented. Smokers tend to wrinkle earlier, probably because smoking has a drying effect on the system and the fact that cigarette smoke contains formaldehyde, the same chemical used by pathologists to preserve or pickle specimens. Smoking can make a woman look and feel older than she would otherwise.

If you smoke to keep your weight down, you may be successful in keeping an extra five pounds off, but the trade-off may be that you will age faster, have more lines on your face and have less energy. If smoking is going to make you look older, isn't that defeating the purpose?

For some women, entering menopause can be disturbing and stressful. If you can think of this time in your life as a new beginning, you will find quitting smoking much easier. If you mourn the childbearing years and feel that menopause is an end to your youth and vitality forever, you will be greatly distressed when you realize that you are going through "the change."

The perimenopausal phase can be a confusing time. It's that gray area where you aren't sure whether you are experiencing PMS or premenopausal symptoms. Again, there can be wild fluctuations in hormone levels, which can create disturbing physical and emotional symptoms.

Women in Western countries usually stop ovulating at about the age of 51. We used to think of menopause as a very sudden event. The ovaries, however, start producing less estrogen in the mid-thirties. Menopausal symptoms often start to occur in the forties and some women have them as early as in their thirties. Increasingly, American women going to menopause clinics are younger by four or five years than in the recent past. The number of younger women with all the symptoms of menopause, even though they still have periods, has been underestimated.

You can start to feel restless and cranky for no reason. As membranes become drier, you can experience a reduction in libido. When you start having night sweats and hot flashes you may become frightened that your youth is slipping away and that you will become old overnight.

If you are in your thirties, forties or fifties and are experiencing any menopausal symptoms, it's imperative that you see a gynecologist. Hormone replacement therapy not only can relieve your symptoms now, it can help you to stay youthful looking, avoid or lessen osteoporosis and restore any diminished libido. Again, you should carefully choose your doctor to be sure that she or he is up-to-date on the latest treatments.

Some women prefer a female gynecologist as women doctors are often more sensitive to the particular needs of each individual woman. Many of the best gynecologists, however, will not accept patients who are not willing to participate actively in their own health care or who smoke. If you choose such a doctor, tell her that you are actively working on breaking your smoking addiction and know that it will be easier if your PMS or menopausal symptoms are relieved.

The diet for premenopause and menopause is similar to the one for PMS, except that as a woman enters her premenopausal phase she should increase her calcium intake. Again, it should always be balanced with magnesium because, without magnesium, calcium cannot be properly absorbed.

The very things that make women such warm, nurturing, sensitive human beings can cause us pain when we get older and as our children get out into the world more and need us less. So much emphasis is put on youth and body-shape, that as we age and put on a few pounds, we feel less desirable. Simply growing older can cause stress in many women.

This is the time for you to get every book you can get your hands on that will help you through this time. Until you read what other women have gone through you may not believe that this can be the most beautiful time of life for you. Two excellent books on menopause are *The Change: Women, Aging and the Menopause* by Germaine Greer and *The Silent Passage* by Gail Sheehy. Both have been around for awhile, but I have found no better books on this subject.

Menopause does not need to be a time to start winding down your life. This can be the opportunity you've been waiting for to truly take control of your life. If you take positive actions such as increase your exercise, improve your diet, get hormonal replacement therapy when indicated, and search for deeper meanings in your life, this can be a time of magnificent transformation.

How and what you eat can affect your mood

How and what you eat play a very big part in maintaining a normal hormone balance. By adjusting your diet during your cycle, you can avoid the disturbing mood swings that make it so much harder to remain a nonsmoker.

It is not natural for women to be pencil thin. And, more and more, we are discovering that it also isn't healthy. Estrogen is stored in body fat. As we get older and our estrogen levels drop, being thin can bring our estrogen levels even lower. Obesity certainly isn't healthy either, but there is a middle ground. Unfortunately, at a normal, average weight, most women feel fat.

We should have soft, round places on our bodies. At other times in history, voluptuous, Rubenesque women were considered the image of beauty. It is important for us to love ourselves no matter what shape our body is in. Having a good healthy diet, exercising regularly and maintaining a positive outlook on life are far more important to our well-being than trying to look the way some fashion designer or ad campaign depicts as the ideal.

In summary, smoking worsens PMS symptoms and PMS makes it harder for women to quit smoking. The same is true of premenopausal and menopausal symptoms. It all has to do with hormonal balance. Eating a proper diet can help alleviate both PMS and menopausal symptoms. When you are less stressful, it is easier to quit smoking.

Birth control pills and smoking can be a lethal

combination. There may also be a problem for premenopausal and menopausal women who are taking estrogen while they are smoking.

If you are experiencing disturbing physical or psychological symptoms, it is essential that you see your doctor and have a complete physical checkup. It may be very helpful to also get psychological counseling at this time.

In a later chapter, you will be given help in selecting a well-balanced, nutritious diet and in planning low-fat, low-calorie meals that will help you keep your weight down while you are overcoming your addiction to cigarettes. The value of regular exercise will also be discussed.

Chapter 3
Quitting Gradually or "Cold Turkey"

If you have tried to quit several times before but didn't, don't let yourself feel like a failure—rejoice! The good news is that each time you quit you are a little bit closer to being able to quit for good. Quitting is good practice. And even if it weren't, each day you spend breathing good, clean air, untainted by toxic smoke, is one less nail in your coffin. Think of all the times you quit as little successes. Don't think of all the times you started up again as failures. They were merely setbacks. They were practice sessions—and practice makes perfect.

Recently, researchers have found that people who give up smoking by cutting down gradually are more likely to remain nonsmokers. Perhaps the reason is that it's easier physically and emotionally.

At a recent meeting of the American Society of Addiction Medicine a study was presented by John Pierce of the University of California at San Diego. A quit smoking program based on Pierce's findings had enabled 26.7 percent of participating smokers to quit, about twice the rate of those who quit without the program. He found that those who could delay the day's first cigarette or who gave up smoking for seven days had a good chance of eventually dropping the habit for good. The goal was not to get them to quit "cold turkey" but to get them to quit for at least a week or to cut down to under 15 cigarettes a day.

David Abrams of Brown University in Providence, Rhode Island, an authority on smoking cessation, said that the study confirmed an emerging view that quitting is often a gradual process. He stated, "You've got to see a slip or a relapse as a learning process, rather than a failure." Ninety percent of smokers who try to go cold turkey fail to quit, most of them relapsing within four days, Pierce said. In interviews, 4,624 Californians were asked about their smoking habits and history and then interviewed again 18 months later. Of the smokers who had said in the first interview that they had quit for a week, 18 percent had quit altogether by the time of the second interview. Of those who had never quit for a week, only 10 percent had quit by the second interview.

Be glad that you can't smoke at work

The study also found that restriction of smoking at home and in the workplace was a factor contributing to successful quitting, especially when combined with a no-smoking program. So don't be angry when you are sent outside into the cold rain to smoke your cigarette. It really is for your own good.

For most people, quitting "cold turkey" is painful. Many smoking cessation therapists/facilitators, if they are aware of this fact, are reluctant to tell people who are trying to quit that a gradual approach may be better for them. I understand that reluctance because I share their concern that a smoker may delay quitting, using this as an excuse. "I'll just cut down now and quit later," could be just another indication that the nicotine addict is into denial.

For that reason, I suggest that you try to be completely honest with yourself before you choose the gradual approach. It may work for you, or you may be one of those people who absolutely must quit cold turkey if you are to quit at all.

Again, it's your choice. No one can make you quit and no one can do it for you. Only you can decide whether it's best for you to start by cutting down, preparatory to quitting altogether. That's the way I did it.

I had tried over and over to quit. For more than two years before I actually stopped smoking for good I was told by my doctor that I must quit. During the night my hands had been going to sleep. If I reached for a glass of water, I'd often drop it because I couldn't feel it. Then one morning I awoke and my entire leg was asleep. I couldn't feel it and I couldn't move it. With my hands I lifted my leg off the bed, dangling it and massaging it until the sensation came back. That's when I went to the doctor. I also suffered from extremes of both cold and heat. Raynaud's syndrome, a circulatory disorder, was the diagnosis.

There was no cure but, as nicotine is a vasoconstrictor, he told me, I should quit smoking. When I said that I was down to a pack a day and asked how important it *really* was that I quit, my doctor asked me how important my fingers and toes were to me. I got the message but it was two more years before I finally snubbed out my last cigarette.

Although I wasn't able to quit right away, I was able to cut down. I started delaying my first cigarette until after lunch. After awhile I could delay it until after dinner. In about a year's time, I had reduced my smoking to half a pack a day except when I went to a party. A cigarette always went with a drink. I still couldn't break that link. What I should have realized was that drinking alcohol breaks down your resistance and your resolve and it's a lot easier to give in to urges. Although I didn't have the numbness as much as I did before, it still happened. The degree and frequency of numbness was in direct proportion to the number of cigarettes I smoked each day.

I did continue to cut down, though. Sometimes I was able to go all week without a cigarette and then smoke only half of a pack on weekends. But even when I was down to half a pack a week, I was still addicted. I had to have those cigarettes! It wasn't until I got the flu that I was able to quit altogether. That was when I was able to make negative associations with my smoking. More about this in another chapter.

If you quit gradually you must have a plan

If you choose the gradual approach, you must have a plan as to how you are going to do it. Are you going to only smoke on weekends? Are you going to cut down by a few cigarettes a day until you have quit completely? What is your time frame for quitting?

Chapter 3

There are many ways to quit smoking and whatever way works for you is the best way—for you. One fifty-one-year-old woman I know smoked only half a pack a day but was addicted to that half pack. She told me she finally quit but it was in a strange, and expensive, way. She would quit for as much as a few months at a time. Then she would give in and buy a pack of cigarettes. She would then take one out and smoke it and throw the rest of the pack away. She knew that if she kept them, she would smoke them. After three or four tries, she quit altogether.

It wasn't as hard for her as it is for most of us. First of all, she only smoked half a pack a day. Second, she didn't start smoking in the first place until she was 25 years old. However, even at that, she had felt the effects of smoking. It drastically affected her energy level and she was allergic to tobacco smoke. She was able to quit finally when her doctor told her she must.

If you choose to quit gradually, you still must choose a time by which you will have quit altogether and forever. I do not recommend doing it the way I did it. It took two years to do. Knowing what I do now about the health consequences of smoking, I believe that you should make a decision to quit entirely in a month or less.

A. Choose the right time of the month to begin your program

If you no longer have menstrual periods, plan to start your stop smoking program on the first day of the month. If you are menstruating then begin cutting down one week before your period. This is your premenstrual phase when you may be experiencing PMS symptoms. Remember, you will not be quitting right away and even though you may be feeling increased stress, you need to make the commitment at this time. You will need to build the confidence in yourself that you can quit even though you are at a low ebb in your monthly cycle.

B. Maintain a daily log

When you choose this way of quitting it is imperative that you follow this program to the letter. Maintain a daily log. Take a small notebook with you wherever you go and pull it out every time you have a cigarette. Write down every cigarette you smoke, the time of day or night you smoke it and what you are feeling that causes you to light up.

This serves several purposes. It keeps you aware of every cigarette you smoke so that you can't just smoke automatically. It helps you realize what is going on in your own subconscious mind by forcefully bringing it out into your conscious thinking. You can discover by looking back in your log after several days what it is that makes you feel you must have a cigarette. You will find a pattern emerging and will learn what specific events and thoughts prompt your smoking more than others. This is valuable to know in dealing with your ability to remain a nonsmoker once you reach that point.

One other thing: smoking has become a hassle. The more your habit becomes a hassle, the easier it will be to quit. When it stops being fun, there is more reason to give it up altogether. Among the women who have the most trouble quitting, or who don't even try, the reason they give is that they "enjoy it." Keeping a log of every cigarette you smoke will surely help take away that sense of enjoyment.

You may be thinking that you don't want to give up this pleasure but, again, remember that the pleasure you feel is the addiction talking. Skydiving is undoubtedly fun, too, but if you do it without a parachute, it's deadly. There is no parachute for smoking. There is no known protection from the damaging effects. It may take longer than skydiving to feel the effects, but it is still most certainly a killer. To ignore this fact is to remain in denial.

When you are taking the gradual approach to smoking cessation, the number of cigarettes you smoke each day is related to how much you normally smoke. Adjust the number according to how you smoke.

C. Cut down on the number of cigarettes you smoke each day

If you are currently smoking two packs or more a day, cut down to one pack a day for the next week. If you normally smoke one pack, cut down to a half a pack. Cutting your consumption in half right away may not seem gradual to you but, unless you want to stretch out your time to quit over several months, it is the best way. The following plan is based on a two-pack-a-day habit.

If you buy your cigarettes by the carton, take out seven packs and put the rest away where you can't get to them easily. That way, if you go over a pack in any one day, you'll have to adjust the next day by smoking less than a pack.

During week two, cut down to a half-pack a day. Follow the same regime as above. Continue to maintain your log. On the third week, you should be down to five cigarettes a day. That's less than two packs of cigarettes for the week. Count them out and don't go over that amount. By the fourth week, allow yourself only one pack of cigarettes for the entire week. That's just less than three cigarettes a day. Unless you decided to do this in February, you have two or three days left in the month. Allow yourself one cigarette each day.

At the end of the month, throw away any cigarettes you have left. Make a pact with yourself never to smoke again. Tell everyone you know that you have quit. Continue reading the rest of the book for help in remaining a nonsmoker.

If this works for you, great! But if you cheat at all on this program, you must decide to go cold turkey. That may be a little harder for you to do but you might be the type of person who has to do it that way if they're to do it at all. Whichever way you choose, read on...

Chapter 4

Remove the Blocks and Change Your Mind

Although half of the smokers in the United States today are women, that is a recent development. Before World War II, it was rare to find a woman who smoked. It was considered unladylike.

A brief history of tobacco

The use of tobacco originated among the aborigines in the Western Hemisphere in pre-Columbian times. Originally tobacco was used in religious rituals and in some instances for medicinal purposes. Tobacco was introduced into Spain and Portugal in the sixteenth century by the explorers of the New World. It spread to other European countries and then to Asia and Africa. However, many rulers of that time prohibited its use and penalized offenders. "Herein is not only a great vanity, but a great contempt of God's good gifts, that the sweetness of man's breath, being a good gift of God, should be willfully corrupted by this stinking smoke... a custom loathsome to the eye, hateful to the nose, harmful to the brain, dangerous to the lungs, and in the black, stinking fume thereof nearest resembling the horrible Stygian smoke of the pit that is bottomless." James I of England (c. 1620) Even then, many people realized the health hazards of smoking. And that was long before many of the questionable additives were incorporated into cigarettes by modern manufacturers.

The health hazards of tobacco use have been suspected for almost 400 years. The first reported clinical impressions of a relationship between tobacco and disease date from the eighteenth century, when tobacco use was associated with lip and nasal cancers. It was only in this century that a true understanding of the health effects of tobacco came into being. In 1920 an article in the *Journal of the American Medical Association* linked tobacco use to lip cancer. The *New England Journal of Medicine* published an article in 1928 noting that heavy smoking was more common among cancer patients than in a control group. In 1938 it was noted in the journal *Science* that heavy smokers had a shorter life expectancy. In the late 1940s and early 1950s scientific studies strongly linked smoking to lung cancer.

Public Enemy Number One

Every one of the last five Surgeons General of the U.S. Public Health Service has identified cigarette smoking as one of the nation's most significant sources of death and disease. On June 1, 1961, the presidents of the American Cancer Society, the American Public Health Association, the American Heart Association and the National Tuberculosis Association (now the American Lung Association) urged President John F. Kennedy to form a commission to study the health consequences of smoking. An advisory committee was

Chapter 4

established in 1962 and their final report was released on January 11, 1964.

In it they stated that, "Cigarette smoking is causally related to lung cancer in men; the magnitude of the effect of cigarette smoking far outweighs all other factors. The data for women, though less extensive, point in the same direction. The risk of developing lung cancer increases with duration of smoking and the number of cigarettes smoked per day, and is diminished by discontinuing smoking." The advisory committee concluded that "Cigarette smoking is a health hazard of sufficient importance in the United States to warrant appropriate remedial action."

Warning labels and the tobacco lobby

The Federal Trade Commission then proposed that cigarette packs and advertisements bear warning labels and that strict limitations be placed on the content of cigarette advertising. Congress, however, preempted the FTC's recommendation and, beginning in 1966, a congressionally mandated health warning appeared on all cigarette packs but not on advertisements.

Thanks to the powerful tobacco lobby, tobacco advertising and promotion has continued. Cigarettes are one of the most heavily marketed consumer products in the United States. Cigarette advertising and promotional expenditures totaled 2.4 billion dollars in 1986 (the last year for which data are available). Cigarettes are the most heavily advertised category of products in the outdoor media (billboards), the second most heavily advertised category in magazines (after passenger cars) and the third most heavily advertised subcategory in newspapers (after passenger cars and airlines). All six of the major cigarette manufacturers were included among the 100 companies with the highest advertising expenditures in 1985.

According to FTC reports, the major advertising themes associated cigarette smoking with high-style living, healthy activities, and economic, social and professional success. Everyone would want to identify with those themes. They are especially appealing to women, who still earn only about 65 to 70 cents to every dollar of what men earn—and more especially to lower socio-economic girls and women. This latter group is the most rapidly expanding group of smokers in this country.

Cigarette advertising

Advertising campaigns for Virginia Slims and Eve cigarettes, of course, targeted young women and were highly effective. Cigarette smoking rose dramatically in girls and young women after these ads were initiated. A paper in an April 1994 issue of the *Journal of the American Medical Association* reported these findings by researchers of the University of California at San Diego. They had discovered that, although the smoking rates of teenage girls rose very little between World War II and 1967, they skyrocketed when ads started pitching brands like Virginia Slims and Eve to women. Between 1967 and 1973 the rate of smoking for 12-year-old girls shot up 110 percent! The Tobacco Institute claims that the increased smoking among girls coincided with women's lib and the incidence of bra-burning.

Most health researchers believe that education about the health hazards of smoking would result in fewer people starting to smoke and more smokers quitting. They conclude that knowledge and attitude changes evolve into reductions in smoking. However, many women's magazines that carry cigarette ads are reluctant to publish articles covering the hazards of tobacco for fear of losing advertising revenues. Women have thus been deprived of information that might have improved their knowledge of the particular damage to women of smoking.

In a study of 10 prominent women's magazines that carry cigarette advertisements, researchers found that four had carried no antismoking articles in the entire 12-year period between 1967 and 1979. The other magazines had published from 12 to 63 times as many articles on individual topics such as nutrition, contraception, stress and mental health as they did on the antismoking theme. Between 1972 and 1981, *Ms. Magazine's* cigarette advertising revenue was 14.8 percent of their total ad revenue. During that time, *Ms.* did not carry one single article on smoking. Neither did *Redbook* between 1970 and 1981, and their cigarette advertising revenue was 16.1 percent of their total ad revenue. Whose interests are these magazines looking out for?

In a recent issue of *Self* there were several articles on health. One was about doctors overmedicating women. Another was on eating eight healthy servings of grains a day. Two were on exercise and one was on the potential dangers of cooking in aluminum, copper and stainless steel pans. There was even an article on getting a tan from a bottle rather than risking exposing the skin to cancer-causing rays of the sun. There was not one article about smoking. However, there was a two-page, centerfold ad for "Classic Capri Super Slims" cigarettes. It showed a young, very slender woman holding a cigarette with a caption across the top of the page stating, "There is no slimmer way to smoke."

Advertising is powerful. There are subliminal as well as obvious messages carefully designed to make us want the products or services advertised. Smoke Virginia Slims and you will be slim, beautiful, popular and prosperous. The women in the ads are. The women are also athletic and well dressed. They are young and happy. The message is "that could be you if you smoke these cigarettes." Does it make sense? No, of course not. We know that—at least consciously, we know that. But this propaganda doesn't work on the conscious mind. It works on the subconscious.

To counteract this type of mind corruption, you, too, have to work on the subconscious mind. You must realize that you started smoking because something inside you believed that smoking would make you look more sophisticated, more mature, more appealing. You probably practiced the way to hold a cigarette, even watched yourself in the mirror when you smoked those first few cigarettes to be sure that you looked good doing it. The way you put the cigarette to your mouth and inhaled, then blew the smoke out slowly said to the world, "Look at me, I'm self-assured. I'm cool."

Chapter 4

When I was a little girl and I saw Paul Henried light two cigarettes in his mouth and hand one to Bette Davis in *Now Voyager*, I wanted some handsome man to do that for me someday. It was so romantic. The powerful, independent women in the movies always seemed to smoke. The cigarette was a symbol of their freedom. It showed that they were in control; they were in charge of their own life. I watched the beautiful, exciting women on the screen look into the leading man's eyes as he lit their cigarettes. Their eyes would lock in an animal hunger for each other. Whew! I could hardly wait until I was old enough to smoke.

Unfortunately, depicting smoking in a favorable light in films continues. Brown & Williamson Tobacco Corporation spent more than $950,000 in a span of four years to feature its cigarettes in more than 20 movies. According to the Los Angeles Times, a Sylvester Stallone film received $300,000. Films in which Paul Newman and Sean Connery appeared also reportedly were paid to include smoking scenes. These payments for the display of brand-name merchandise in films is legal. It is a potentially large source of revenue for filmmakers.

How long had you been smoking before you realized that you had been had by the tobacco companies? How long before you knew that you were destroying your health? If you're reading this now, you are no longer into denial. You are ready to take back control of your own mind and regain your health before you reach the point of no return.

Change your thinking habits

How do you do this? The first thing you must learn to do is to start changing some of your thinking habits. Do not refer to yourself as a smoker. When it comes to negative actions, *never confuse what you do with who you are.* If you have ever run a red light or exceeded the speed limit, you may have broken the law but you would hardly consider yourself a criminal. Beginning now, *stop calling yourself a smoker.* You are simply a person who, at the present time, smokes cigarettes.

At one time in your life, you may have used a pacifier or sucked your thumb. You may have bitten your fingernails. I bit my nails until I was 16 (about the same time that I started smoking). Many, if not most people who smoke, did do one or more of the above in their early lives. Most people gave up those childhood things with time. That was just a phase they went through.

You might find it helpful to think of your smoking as *just a phase you are going through*. You can start right now thinking about how long you will allow it to last before you "phase it out" for good. More about this in a later chapter.

I was finally able to quit for good because I changed my thinking about smoking. Not my conscious thinking. I knew consciously that it was bad for me. I realized that I had to change my *unconscious* thinking.

Be determined to quit for good

To stop smoking and remain a nonsmoker for the rest of your life, you must reach the point of *knowing in every part of your being* that to be in control of your health—of your very life—you must stop smoking. You must also believe not only that you can but that you will.

The decision must be made and then you must become determined to make it happen. You must love yourself enough to give yourself the great gift of good health. No one deserves it more than you do.

Nicotine gum and the nicotine transdermal patch

At this point, I want to discuss nicotine gum and the nicotine patch. I know that many people have used them to overcome the initial difficulties of quitting smoking. I have known people who have said that without that extra help they couldn't have stayed off cigarettes. But I, personally, don't believe they should be used.

There are two reasons I discourage them. The first is that they may help you at first in reducing your cravings for nicotine, but when you stop using them, the cravings come back. You never really overcame your addiction to nicotine; you were just taking it in a different form. To remain a nonsmoker, you must learn to do it without using crutches.

The second reason is that I think they are unsafe, especially the nicotine patch. I have known several incidents of people smoking while wearing the patch and having a stroke or a heart attack. There have been cases of people having heart attacks even if they did not smoke while wearing the patch. I have heard of a couple of people who died. The delivery of nicotine into the bloodstream is not regulated when you wear the patch as it is when you smoke a cigarette.

When you smoke *and* use the patch, you get a double dose of nicotine and it can be deadly. For some reason these stories never seem to make it into the news.*

Shortly after the patch was introduced, sales soared to the highest levels ever seen for a new pharmaceutical product. They were $270 million in one quarter alone. But sales dropped with the realization that the patch is not a panacea. The success rates of smoking cessation using the patch have, in fact, been dismal. The process of overcoming the addiction to smoking is extremely complex, pharmacologically, socially and psychologically.

Smokers, wanting an easy way out of their addiction, responded in unprecedented numbers at the beginning. Brilliant consumer advertising touted the patch as a miracle treatment. First quarter sales were so high that supplies of the Marion Merrell Dow "Nicoderm" patch ran out. Other manufacturers jumped on the bandwagon and brought out their own versions. By the end of 1992, however, sales had plummeted at least 50 percent. Most of the 5 million people who tried the patch had still not been able to quit smoking.

Michael Samuelson, president of the National Center for Health Promotion, believes that considering the patch to be a "magic pill" is "ludicrous and dangerous." He states that "Patches can only be effective if they are used with a medical component, a

---

*Pregnant women, especially, should not use the nicotine patch. The effects on the fetus of this type of nicotine delivery system has not been determined.

strong behavior component and, most important, a sincere desire to stop smoking."

Again, motivation and determination absolutely have to be there for anyone to have any long-lasting success in quitting.

Some case histories

Recently I met with three women who had completed a stop-smoking program four months before. One of them was a woman whom I will call Bonnie who had smoked a pack and a half a day for 20 years. For the first time in her life she had stayed off cigarettes for longer than two or three weeks. But then she started again when her daughter was getting a divorce. As she was trying to comfort her inconsolable daughter, who between sobs was puffing incessantly, she broke down and asked for a cigarette. Her daughter tried to talk her out of it, but Bonnie grabbed her cigarettes and started smoking again that night. Bonnie, feeling powerless to help her child in her time of need, also felt powerless over her addiction. She had never stopped wanting a cigarette. The class helped her to get started on breaking the addiction, but her unconscious mind had never accepted the fact that she could quit for good.

Marcia had quit because her husband had begged her to. She was older than he and had been married before. She was the love of his life and he feared that she wouldn't be around to share their golden years if she continued to smoke. Not yet 40, Marcia was already showing signs of damage from smoking. She wheezed, coughed a lot and had chest pains. She loved her husband very much and wanted to please him. She also knew that she *should* quit.

Marcia was doing okay until she went back East for a family reunion. Her husband hadn't been able to go because he couldn't leave his job. At every get-together it seemed like everyone in her large, Italian family was smoking. She joined in the celebrating, singing, laughing and drinking, and by the second day, she had also joined them in smoking. She had never quit for as long as three months before and until that fateful reunion she thought that she had finally kicked it for good.

When she returned, she didn't tell her husband that she was smoking again. She was sneaking around to smoke. She'd stand under the range hood over the stove, turn on the exhaust fan and blow her smoke out. She'd go into the back yard on some pretense and light up. Before she'd kiss her husband, she'd brush her teeth and wash her hands. He never guessed, she said. She was afraid that if he did, he'd divorce her. She insisted that it didn't seem to be hurting her physically. We reminded her of her coughing and chest pains. Then she said, "Well, they really don't bother me much and I don't know if that has anything to do with my smoking. I'm really only trying to quit for my husband's sake."

When asked what was the single most difficult thing to overcome in trying to quit, she said that she just enjoys smoking too much. However, she was never able to explain exactly what it was about smoking that she enjoyed.

Several things made it almost a certainty that Marcia wouldn't be able to stay off cigarettes. First, she wasn't doing it for herself. Second, she was convinced that she enjoyed it and third, she kept telling herself that it was doing her no harm. This is a classic case of someone who is unable to face the truth when it comes to smoking. Marcia was heavily into denial. She wasn't just lying to her husband, she was lying to herself.

The easier way

Donna was the only one of the three who was still not smoking. The key was that she had done it the easy way. She didn't feel deprived. She had done it for herself and she believed that, next to giving birth to a beautiful baby boy, it was probably the most successful thing she'd ever done in her life. She said that she is absolutely determined never to smoke again. She spoke of how good she feels about herself and how much more energy she now has. Even when she's around other people who are smoking she said she is never tempted. She is very honest about her feelings and she is aware of the fact that she alone is responsible for whether she smokes or not. She admits that she cried some at first and that she sometimes thinks about cigarettes even now, but she can't imagine anything that could possibly happen which would get her to smoke again.

She has had some difficult times to face since she quit smoking. She had recently been laid off and, being a single parent of a pre-teen, was concerned about how she was going to support him. Although she was having trouble paying her bills, she was cheerful and positive about the future. She spoke about how much better she feels, how all of her senses are more intense. Food tastes better, she has more endurance, her clothes don't smell bad anymore, she doesn't have ugly yellow stains on her fingers. She went on and on enumerating the ways in which her life had improved, her skin was clearer, her nails didn't break as easily, even the little lines around her mouth and eyes seemed to have diminished. She said she feels more alive now than she can ever remember.

Donna had done it the easy way. Not only did she not feel deprived, she believed that she was giving herself a wonderful gift. She never thought that she was doing it for her son, although her son was delighted. She knew she was doing it for herself. Her attitude was completely different from the attitudes of the ones who were smoking again.

Recently I spoke to a woman who had been in my stop-smoking program a year and a half ago. Shirley had attended the sessions because she had never been able to quit smoking on her own for longer than a few days at a time. But, at that time, she knew she must quit because she had to undergo surgery, and her doctor told her he would not operate until she had been a nonsmoker for at least a month. He refused to put her under the deep anesthesia that was required for the surgery unless her lungs were clear. He felt it was too hazardous.

Although she didn't appear that heavy, Shirley told me later that when she had gone through the stop-smoking program she weighed over 200 pounds. After her surgery, her weight shot up to over 250 pounds. She attributed the weight gain both to the long recuperative period when she was not physically active and to her quitting smoking. Still she was determined not to let that give her an excuse to start smoking again. As her strength returned she started exercising and following the diet she had learned in the program. She had continued doing her relaxation and visualization exercises because she knew that it could also help her heal faster.

As she was recovering, she saved the money she would have spent on cigarettes. When she was fully recovered she went back to school full time and the money she had saved paid her tuition and for her books. Prior to her surgery she had been an accountant and, although she made good money, she hated it. After attending classes in a local college for a year, she started earning a living as a graphic artist—her lifelong dream. She also lost 100 pounds and believes that she looks better than she ever has in her life. She certainly feels better.

Shirley attributed the drastic change in her life mainly to finally breaking her smoking addiction. She believed that if she could quit smoking, she could do anything—and then she set about to prove it!

As a smoking cessation therapist, you never know what it is that's going to work with an individual smoker. I asked her what was the main reason for her success. She told me that first of all it was her strong desire to quit. That has to be there for any program to work.

Nothing will help a smoker who is not truly dedicated to making an effort to quit. Then, she said, it was the support and the attention she received both from me and from the group. It was important for her to know someone cared about her.

Shirley was surprised that there wasn't the pain she had previously felt when she had tried to quit smoking. When she got back onto the stop-smoking diet, remembering to eat small portions every three or four hours and starting to lose weight, it was easier to resist smoking. Shirley also recalled that she had learned that she might have a desire for a cigarette during stressful times, so she wasn't thrown off when those times occurred. She reminded herself that the urge, no matter how strong, would pass within seconds and all she had to do was wait it out. At first she would have to wait for over a minute, but as time went on, it became only seconds until her mind was off cigarettes and onto something else. Shirley realized that a cigarette might momentarily calm her down at stressful times, but the calmness would last only seconds and then she would be more nervous than before.

She reports that she now feels more tranquil and at peace than she ever has. Gone is the panic of being out of cigarettes when she might "need" one. As she had a three- to three-and-a-half-pack-a-day habit, she saved a great deal of money over time.

Shirley walks every day, eats a well-balanced diet that includes fresh fruits and vegetables, takes a Yoga class, meditates and works at a job she loves. Using the excuse of weight gain to put off quitting smoking is simply a cop-out, she says. She was very overweight when she was a smoker, and now that she is a non-smoker she is a normal size. People who smoke are not necessarily thin and people who don't are not necessarily overweight. There all kinds of sizes and shapes within each group.

Shirley's success story so impressed me that I have asked her to come and speak to my stop-smoking groups. And she has happily agreed to.

Filling the void with something better

Believing that you are giving yourself a gift by not smoking, I knew, was the key. As long as you feel that you are giving up something you love and have not replaced it with something better, you will feel pain. Perhaps most important of all is learning to be honest with yourself. For, as long as you lie to yourself or to anybody else, you will probably not be able to quit smoking for good. Even if you do, through willpower, you will miss it and may never get over that desire for a cigarette. This is definitely the hard way. And totally unnecessary.

The point Donna and Shirley reached can be reached by anyone. It is simply a matter of reprogramming your thought patterns. By getting it through to your unconscious mind that smoking is not a pleasure and cigarettes are not friends, you *can give up smoking without pain.*

We all have at least two people inside us. Our adult self and our child. That physical, conscious part of us is our adult. The unconscious, that dreamy, creative, emotional part of us, is our child. The conscious part of us is the sensible self that gets us to work, teaches us to drive a car, pays our bills and takes care of the business side of our life. But this conscious part of us is often in conflict with our own unconscious mind, like an authoritarian parent who tries to control a willful child who keeps running away or just wants to play.

Habits and addictions are learned behaviors, and usually they start in the conscious part of us. You consciously lit that first cigarette and pulled the smoke into your mouth and then into your lungs. You learned how to smoke either from watching others or from someone coaching you. You learned to feed yourself and to drink from a cup the same way. Now they are all "automatic." You don't have to think about them. How many times have you lighted a cigarette and taken several puffs before you realized you had done it? I can remember being so unconscious about smoking that I would light a cigarette while I still had one burning in the ashtray.

The wayward child within us

If you are to quit smoking once and for all, it isn't your conscious mind you have to convince. You may have done that already. If you want a child to listen, you don't talk to his/her parent. You must get to the child, in this case, your unconscious mind, and convince it that it wants to do whatever is necessary to be healthy. You must convince the little girl within you that smoking is *not* fun. Doing things that are harmful to the body or mind are *not* enjoyable. That child must feel that it's more fun to be good than it is to be bad. There is greater joy in being healthy and in control than there is in running amok.

If you are still smoking when you know that you shouldn't, your wayward child is in control. If you scold that little girl and try to control her, you'll only get rebellion. She might behave while you're there, but as soon as your back is turned she will go back to her old ways. That child has to believe that it is doing what it wants to do. That is the only way you will get lasting results.

So how do you get to the unconscious mind? You show it how to have *healthy* fun. You teach it new habits. You break the old ones. But first, you have to get its attention. Your unconscious may not like it at first, but it must learn that you know what is best. So you must start by taking away those attractive nuisances, temptations, toys—in this case, cigarettes.

Three Things You Must Do Now
1. Throw away all your cigarettes, lighters, matches, cigarette cases and ashtrays. Get them out of your sight. Get them out of your house, your office, your workshop, your car.

2. Tell your smoking friends and relatives (if you can) that although you love them, you can't be around them right now. Let them know what you are doing and ask them for their help. Tell them that if you ever ask for a cigarette they are not, under any circumstances, to give you one.

3. Avoid places where there are smokers. Go only to nonsmoking restaurants. There are lots of them now.

Your child isn't going to be too happy when you take away her toys. She's going to get irritable. She may cry or lash out at everyone around her. Maybe you'll get lucky and she won't. But most likely the little girl in you will be in conflict with the adult you and want to regain control. But that is *your child*, remember. If she wanted to run out into the street and into traffic, would you let her? Would you give her back her toy if her toy were a time bomb? Of course not. You love your child and want to take care of her. Retrain that child if you want her to take good care of you, too, in your later years. As Captain Cuttle, a character from Charles Dickens once said, "Train up a fig-tree in the way it should go, and when you are old sit under the shade of it."

TWO POWERFUL WAYS TO RETRAIN YOUR CHILD (UNCONSCIOUS MIND)

1. To break a bad habit or addiction, teach "your child" to associate it with something extremely abhorrent.

2. To create a new, healthy pattern of thinking, practice associating good habits with great pleasure.

In the following chapters, I will explain in detail how to work with your subconscious mind so that it will make negative associations with smoking and positive associations with clear, smokeless breathing.

Chapter 5
Get in Touch With Yourself

Just as there are reasons you started smoking, there are reasons you are still smoking. Yes, you are addicted, that's true. But lots of people were addicted to nicotine and yet were able to quit smoking. Psychoanalysis hasn't proven to be effective in helping people break their smoking addiction, although it has often been valuable in helping them identify their problems and work on solving them.

This book is not about healing all psychological wounds. That is for the experts. If you are feeling overwhelmed by disturbing emotions, you should consider getting professional help. This book is about overcoming your desire and need to smoke.

You don't have to be crazy or even neurotic to be hooked on cigarettes. It is, after all, a physiological as well as a psychological addiction. And it strikes people from all walks of life, all colors and socio-economic conditions. Poor people, rich people, educated or illiterate, male or female, devoutly religious or atheistic, married or single—it doesn't matter. Smoking is an equal opportunity addiction.

What drives your addiction?

What can help, though, is discovering what it is

in you, yourself, that drives your addiction. It is important to get in touch with your feelings about smoking. Ask yourself the following questions:

- What do you feel when you light a cigarette? Do you light up out of habit? Is it usually a reaction to a stimulus such as stress, anger, frustration or boredom? Are you always aware of lighting and smoking a cigarette? Do you feel guilty every time? Are you fatalistic about your health and mortality? Do you worry about the harm smoking is doing to you? Do you feel like you are giving yourself a reward?

- What do you feel whenever you think about quitting? Does the thought trigger fear, regret, worry? What is the emotion? Can you get to the heart of it? Do you fear that you will fail if you try to quit and you will then think less of yourself? Do you think that you will feel a sense of loss like the regret of having to give up a good friend? Do you worry about gaining weight?

- What did you feel when you cut down or quit in the past? Did you feel good about yourself? Did you feel that something was missing in your life?

- What were you feeling when you increased your smoking or started smoking again after having quit for a time? Can you remember what was happening in your life at the time?

- How do you feel when someone nags you about your smoking? Is there anything anyone could say to you about your smoking that you wouldn't take offense at? Do you want to rebel even more when someone tells you that you should quit? Do you think or maybe even say, "Don't tell me what to do!"

- How do you feel when you are told that you can't smoke in a particular place? Does it make you angry, resentful, sad, panicky? Do you feel like an outcast?

- How do you feel about yourself in general? Do you like yourself? Do you think you are worth taking good care of your health? Are you generally proud of your accomplishments? Do you feel like you are in control of your life?

- How do you think you would feel about yourself if you quit smoking for good? Would you feel more in control of your own destiny? Would you feel a sense of accomplishment?

- What do you think other people's perceptions of you, as a smoker, are? Do you feel that they think less of you because you smoke? Do you believe that they will admire you for quitting?

- What feelings would get in the way of your quitting smoking and remaining a nonsmoker?

How you answer these questions has a great deal to do with whether you have a good chance of quitting smoking forever. Generally, people who have a healthy respect for themselves and an optimistic outlook on their lives find it easier to overcome their nicotine addiction. Also, physically healthy people are more likely to stop smoking than people with a chronic illness. It would seem that it would be the other way around but, unfortunately, it isn't.

Right now, get a pen or pencil and write the answers to the above questions. From time to time, as you read this book, review your answers. As you begin to rethink your beliefs about smoking and your role in molding your own future, you will find that your answers to those questions will change. As you become more in touch with the beauty and strength inside yourself, you will answer many of the questions in a much more positive way.

Instead of feeling scared of being without your friend, the cigarette, when you think about quitting, you may see a bright, healthy future ahead of you. You may start thinking of cigarettes as scary rather than comforting.

Be grateful for being nagged

Instead of feeling angry or rebellious when someone nags you about your smoking, you may feel grateful that someone cares enough about you to want you to be healthy and free. Where you once felt like saying to that friend or loved one, "Don't tell me what to do," you will want to say that to cigarettes. One woman who came to me for help said, "I'm just tired of cigarettes bossing me around!"

Keeping in touch with your feelings and understanding yourself can get you to stop reaching for a cigarette simply out of force of habit. Breaking that automatic response is essential to maintaining your nonsmoking status.

The mind/body connection

There is increasing interest in mind/body medicine. The awareness of the mind/body connection can help people overcome chronic pain, depression, recurrent illnesses, allergies, stress—and addictions. Bill Moyers' book, *Healing and the Mind*, based on the PBS series, is an excellent reference on the healing connections between our minds and our bodies.

Ancient medical science and philosophers of old told us that our minds and bodies are one. That fact is never so clear when we consider addictions. At the time we started smoking it seemed like an appropriate thing to do, whatever our reasons were. It helped us fit into a specific group or made us feel more grown-up and in charge of our own lives at a time when we were emerging from a childhood dependency on our parents.

As the addictive qualities of cigarettes invaded our bodies, they became a part of us. Every cell in our bodies contained nicotine. Within a short time it was difficult to determine whether the addiction was a mental or a physical one. In fact, it was—and is—both. Our brains may be contained in our skull, but our minds are in every part of our body. Yet most of us grew up in a culture that distinctly separates the mind and the body.

We must treat the whole person, not just the addiction

In treating addictions, we must learn to treat the whole person. If we believe that nicotine has only a physical hold on us, we will miss the opportunity to work with our minds in healing this addiction. If we believe it is all in the mind, we will overlook the physical component. That is why there will never be a medication that we can take that will "cure" us of our addiction. And we all know that it isn't enough just to know that smoking is bad for us and we should quit. To be successful we must pay attention to the effects smoking has on our bodies, minds and spirits.

In overcoming our urges to smoke, we must treat all the facets of our "Self." We need to treat our bodies to clean air, to healthy food and to stimulating exercise. We must treat our minds to uplifting thoughts, positive outlooks and respect. We must take into consideration our souls or higher selves or whatever you want to call that part of us that is our spirit.

Keep all this in mind as you review the questions posed above. One woman who told me her story about smoking said that when she quit, it changed her whole life. She explained that what she had learned in the stop-smoking program gave her the tools to take control of other things in her life. Having successfully conquered that hurdle, she became more self-assured, developed more self-esteem and felt stronger than she ever had before. She felt that if she could quit smoking, she could do anything.

Take charge of your emotions.

Once you learn where the emotional buttons are and what feelings they trigger, you can begin to take over the controls. There are several things you can do to manage your emotions and take back your power over your own feelings and actions. Here are some tools you can use:

- Acknowledge and appreciate all of your feelings. Think of them as neither right nor wrong. Do not resist them. You can resist the temptation to smoke without resisting the feelings your addiction calls up.

- Recognize your feelings as being there to support you in making positive changes in your life.

- Think of how you would like to *feel* in troubling or stressful situations. Then practice feeling that way.

- Ask yourself what you would have to believe in order to change your negative feelings.

- Recall a time when you were successful in changing a similar emotion into a positive action.

- Visualize yourself handling future negative feelings in a positive, successful way.

In searching for new material for this book, I looked at literally hundreds of studies and reports by state, county and federal governments as well as medical and scientific groups. Certain patterns emerged, the most notable of which was the wide difference in the way smoking affects men and women. But there is also a difference in its effects on various groups in the population. For instance, Latinos do not appear to become as severely addicted to cigarettes as some of the other groups studied. In searching for reasons for this, the only thing we could find was that Latinos traditionally have very strong family groups. Very often, when one member of a family would enter a stop-smoking program, other members accompanied him or her for support. This support by their loved ones made it easier for the smoker to quit and, most likely, made it less likely for other family members to start smoking.

Enlist the help of your friends and family

What all smokers could learn from this is to enlist the support of your friends and family when you are trying to quit smoking. They can be very helpful in helping you maintain your resolve.

Another fact that the studies showed is that the greater the education, the less likely a person is to smoke. I recently conducted a survey of women and smoking among the members of a professional women's network. Most of the women in the organization have college degrees. Many are medical doctors, psychologists, lawyers or professionals in other fields. Many own their own businesses. As one might guess, only a very small percentage of them are smokers or had ever smoked.

Although the women in the group range in age from 20 to 65 or older, those who participated in the survey ranged from 38 to 62 years old. The questionnaire (see *figure 1*) was given both to those who were presently smoking and to those who had once smoked but had quit. The average age at which this group reported having started smoking was 17.9 years old. The national average is much lower. Many of these women didn't start smoking until they were 20 or 21 and one had started at age 25. The ones who had been successful in quitting had generally started smoking later in life. This study bore out the findings of most of the others, that the earlier one starts to smoke, the harder it is to quit.

figure 1:

WOMEN AND SMOKING — QUESTIONNAIRE

___ I am currently smoking
___ I have stopped smoking

1. I have smoked for ___ years. I am ___ years old.

2. I started smoking when I was ___ years old.

3. I smoke ___ cigarettes per day.

4. I have tried to quit smoking ___ times.
   (Number of attempts)

5. I started again within
   ___ hours ___ days ___ weeks ___ months

6. I have quit smoking for a year or more at a time:
   ___ yes ___ no.

7. I started smoking for the following reason
      (check main reason):
   ___ my friends smoked
   ___ to lose weight
   ___ as an act of rebellion
   ___ to look sophisticated/ sexy/hip

   Other (specify): _____

8. I crave a cigarette when I am (check all that apply):
   ___ lonely   ___ depressed
   ___ happy   ___ angry
   ___ drinking   ___ relaxing
   ___ nervous   ___ fearful
   ___ worried   ___ hungry

   Other: _____

9. I ___ have ___ have not gone through a smoking cessation program.

10. I would like to quit for the following reasons (check all that apply):
    ___ to feel better
    ___ to look better
    ___ for my children/partner/others
    ___ to feel more in control
    ___ my doctor told me to quit

    Other: _____

11. I have not quit for the following reasons (check all that apply):
    ___ fear of weight gain
    ___ fear of failure
    ___ enjoy it too much
    ___ tried and couldn't
    ___ I'm too stressed
    ___ never tried

    Other: _____

12. I believe that I ___ can ___ cannot quit anytime I want to.

13. I believe that it is ___ easier ___ harder for women to quit than it is for men.

14. I believe that most women smoke for the following reasons (check all that apply):
___ stress   ___ rebellion
___ weight control ___ shyness
___ peer pressure   ___ cigarette ad
___ partner smokes

Other: _____

15. This is what it took/would take for me to quit smoking: _____
_____
_____

Other than the age at which both the smokers and ex-smokers had started, there wasn't much difference in the answers between the two groups. In almost all cases they had tried to quit smoking many times. None of them started smoking to lose weight, but several hadn't quit because they were afraid they'd gain weight. In Question 8, "I crave a cigarette when I am (check all that apply)", most of the women checked all of the boxes and added another reason on the line "Other." Fewer than 20 percent had gone through a stop-smoking program.

In Number 11, "I have not quit for the following

reasons... " most of the respondents checked "enjoy it too much" and "I'm too stressed." Clearly, these are the two major items to work with in designing a stop-smoking program.

The greatest challenge for me has been in working with those who say that they enjoy smoking. Usually accompanying that statement is the pronouncement, "...and it's my only vice." This was my mother's reason for not quitting. She used to say to me, "Please don't try to take that pleasure away from me. It is my only self-indulgence." That was true. Mom was the most unselfish person I have ever known.

In my survey, for the most part, there was no evidence of cross-addictions. This is an anomaly I've seen many times in women smokers. Many women who smoke do not seem to have problems with alcohol or other drugs as well. The reverse is not true. Most drinkers or drug abusers also smoke cigarettes.

As stress is pandemic in our society, it is the other major challenge women face in their efforts to quit smoking. Most modern women have to be breadwinners as well as mothers, wives and housekeepers. We expect more of ourselves now than ever before in history. As more and more women are getting out into the working world and struggling to gain a firm foothold on the ladder of success, we are feeling great stress.

To be successful in breaking the smoking addiction then, the two major challenges to be dealt with are (1) the sense that smoking is enjoyable and (2) the stress in our lives.

Chapter 6

Create Negative Associations With Smoking

Teach that child within you (your subconscious) how to think about her toys (cigarettes). Explain the dangers. Whenever she begs for her toys back, show her how destructive those toys are. Every time you find yourself thinking of a cigarette, associate this thought with something painful, disgusting or annoying. If you can associate smoking with something so horrible that you never want to experience it again, you can break your addiction instantly and forever!

Create an aversion to smoking

Have you ever made yourself so sick on some food that you could never eat it again in your life? This happened to me when I was only eleven years old. From the time I was five I had suffered from asthma. Both my mother and stepfather were chain smokers which undoubtedly exacerbated it. My sister and I had gone to the drugstore and gotten root beer floats when I began to feel ill. I left the drugstore and started walking home, but all along the way I had to stop to vomit. We later learned that my asthma had gone into pneumonia and that I was running a high fever. Prior to that incident, root beer was my favorite drink. But to this day I still cannot drink it because I get nauseous even thinking about root beer.

My unconscious mind created that aversion. The incident taught me a very valuable lesson. By remembering this lesson, I finally broke my addiction to cigarettes. It was one of those winters in which everyone it seemed was coming down with a particularly bad strain of the flu. It was the kind where you not only have the headache, fever and chills, but are "running at both ends." It was one of those few times in my life that I didn't particularly care to smoke. The other two times, I'm happy to say, were when I was pregnant. At those times, however, I can remember wanting a cigarette as soon as my babies were born and I was in the recovery room.

As I was suffering the agonies of the flu I started thinking, how can I make this a positive experience? I just wanted to die and was afraid I might not. So I remembered how the very thought of root beer made me feel queasy and realized I might be able to use this experience to associate smoking with feeling awful. Until I got well, every time I had to vomit I visualized myself smoking a cigarette. With each wave of nausea I thought of pulling smoke into my lungs. Over and over I said to myself, "I'm sick because I smoke." Whether or not that was true didn't matter. My unconscious mind didn't know. It just recorded what I told it as fact.

When I recovered I looked at my cigarettes and associated them with feeling ill. At that moment I realized that I could at last give them up. It isn't that I

Chapter 6

never thought of smoking another cigarette again. I did, at times. But they no longer had a hold on me, and I was able to quit—painlessly.

Every time an urge for a cigarette feels overpowering, practice associating it with something you find truly disgusting. Visualize a cigarette floating in wet, putrid garbage. Imagine a sick, toothless, malodorous woman coughing and spitting and puffing on a cigarette butt. Imagine that she could be you in the future. Whenever you think of a cigarette, recall to your mind the pictures you have seen of autopsies of black, damaged lungs. Think of how you would feel if you were trapped in a smoke-filled, burning house and associate that to how you feel inhaling cigarette smoke.

Locate a memory from your past of feeling sick and link that sickness with smoking. Every time you think of smoking, link that thought to something revolting.

Sometimes, putting a rubber band around your wrist and snapping it every time you get an urge to smoke helps create an unpleasant association. You could also pinch yourself and say to yourself, "Smoking hurts."

If you're not ready to give up your cigarettes right now, you can at least start preparing yourself for that time. Make a sign and place it on your package of cigarettes. It could read, "Smoking is dumb. It makes me look stupid." Or "Smoking makes wrinkles." It does, you know. Or how about, "This cigarette will make me sick." Or, "This cigarette will make my stomach hurt." You get the idea. Put a sign on that pack of cigarettes that is the most persuasive to you.

Another thing you can do is wrap a piece of scotch tape around the lower end of each cigarette so that you don't smoke it down to the end. The shorter they are, the more poisonous cigarettes are because there is less to filter the smoke before it reaches you. If you don't want to wrap tape around it, simply draw a line around each cigarette about half-way down. Even if you smoke past the line, you will think about it every time. This creates consistent negative associations with smoking.

Get rid of the excuses and rationalizations

If you find yourself thinking, "Maybe smoking isn't so bad. After all, there are stories of people who smoke living to be a hundred years old. I might be that kind of person." When the cravings come, excuses and rationalizations tag right along. This is when you must replace these rationalizations with *rational realizations*. Reread the first chapter of this book. There is no way to overestimate the hazards of smoking.

Nicotine is toxic

If you need even more ammunition with which to attack your cravings, consider these facts. Nicotine is used as an insecticide. It kills by disrupting the insects' neurotransmitters, the chemicals that link brain cells together. Nicotine operates the same way in *your* body. The next time you think of pulling that hot, toxic smoke into your lungs, think about the havoc it is wreaking. And if you don't care enough about yourself, think of those around you. Secondhand smoke is the *third leading preventable cause of death* in this country. If you are a mother and you smoke around your children, what kind of message are you sending them? Remember, the Environmental Protection Agency has classified secondhand smoke as a Group A carcinogen. That means it is *known to cause cancer in humans*. There is no question. There is no longer any debate. Smoking kills!

The many ways smoking can kill

It kills in a number of different ways. We all know what it does to the smokers' bodies and now we're learning what secondhand smoke does to nonsmokers who are exposed to other people's smoke. But what is rarely mentioned is the numbers of people who die each year from smoke inhalation in fires caused by smoldering cigarettes.

That is how my 25-year-old niece died. Lisa was sweet-natured and beautiful, but troubled. She started smoking when she was 12 and, hanging out with the wrong crowd, started using marijuana shortly afterward. By the time she was 14, she had experimented with cocaine and heroin and became a heroin addict at 16. In and out of treatment centers for years, she had finally seemed to kick heroin.

Her boyfriend, formerly a partner in addiction, had overcome his addiction and had led a productive life for years. Although he had refused to see Lisa until he was comfortable in his own recovery, he did keep in touch. When Lisa had been clean for several months, they got an apartment together and were planning to be married.

Although she had stopped drinking and using drugs, Lisa simply couldn't quit smoking.

One afternoon she fell asleep holding a lighted cigarette in her hand. The cigarette fell between the cushions of the couch she was sitting on and it caught fire. Almost immediately overcome by smoke, Lisa apparently did not wake up. When the fire department found her, she was unconscious. Her burns weren't life-threatening, and she probably would have recovered completely from them. But she had inhaled so much of the toxic fumes from the smoldering couch that she never regained consciousness.

What was particularly tragic was the fact that Lisa seemed to have finally gotten her life together. It seemed ironic that it wasn't illegal drugs that killed her but a legal one.

I recall a particularly bitter winter when I was a teenager living in Washington, D.C. One evening I heard sirens that stopped as the fire trucks screeched to a halt in the street in front of my house. Looking out of the window through the heavy, drifting snow I could see a bright yellow glow in the window of an apartment across the street. The firemen rolled out their hoses and trained it on the window as flames started to lick out of it. Within a few minutes they had the fire out. An ambulance arrived and I saw a fireman come out with a small bundle wrapped in a white sheet with little wisps of smoke emanating from it. When he placed it in the ambulance I realized that it was a body.

The next day I learned that the remains of a large woman were in that small, white package. She had fallen asleep in front of the television and her cigarette had ignited the chair. Before they could reach her, her body had been reduced to unrecognizable charred remains.

There have been many stories of people crashing their cars while lighting a cigarette. How many times have you heard of people dropping their cigarette while driving? I can recall more than once dropping my cigarette between my legs and frantically trying to find it before it burned me. It's easy to lose control of your car during this kind of distraction.

The defensive smoker

Smokers are becoming very defensive. There are few places left to smoke and a lot of antagonism around toward smokers. Recently in San Pablo, California, a 22-year-old mother was convicted of second-degree murder of another woman after an argument in a Denny's restaurant. The killer was a woman who had been sitting in a booth in the restaurant with five children when she lighted up in a nonsmoking section. A woman at an adjoining table asked her to put out her cigarette, and an argument ensued. The smoker left but came back a few minutes later with a gun and blew the complainer away.

The high financial cost of smoking

Even if there were no other negative aspects to smoking, there is the matter of the financial cost of the addiction. A pack-a-day smoker will spend $730 a year on cigarettes at the cost of $2 a pack. If cigarettes go up to $3.50, with a proposed increase in cigarette taxes, that smoker will end up spending nearly $1,300 annually. If she started smoking at 12 or 13, her smoking will have cost her about $65,000 by the time she turns 65. Had she put the money away instead, she would have a nice little nest egg for her retirement years. If she had invested it at an 8 percent annual return, she'd be worth nearly a cool million to warm her golden years.

The real costs of smoking don't stop with the price of cigarettes. Smokers generally pay between 25 percent and 100 percent more for life insurance. They also pay considerably more for auto insurance and for health insurance unless they are covered by a group plan. Add to these the additional costs of medical care, prescriptions and over-the-counter medications. Include the damage to furniture and clothing from cigarette embers as well as the cost of cleaning clothes and drapery and repainting walls and you can see that smoking is indeed an expensive habit.

In an effort to hold down health-care costs, a growing number of private employers are now refusing to hire smokers. Thousands of companies in the United States have forbidden their employees to smoke, even off the job. These companies claim that not hiring smokers not only saves them money but also improves safety conditions, cuts down on absenteeism and minimizes the need to train new employees to replace those who retire early because of heart problems, cancer and emphysema.

A study by the American Lung Association has shown that an employee who smokes can cost a company up to $5,000 a year more in annual insurance premiums than a nonsmoker.

A congressional study in 1990 showed that the direct cost of providing health care to people with smoking-related diseases had reached nearly $21 billion. That figure didn't even include the $7 billion in lost wages for employees who had to take time off because of illness.

What is the cost to you?

The foregoing are some of the negative aspects of smoking. To bring it down to the personal level, think of the cost of smoking to you. Are you paying more for insurance? Have you had to see a doctor for any smoking-related illnesses? Have you ever burned a hole in clothing or furniture? Have you ever spent money on cigarettes that you could ill afford? Have you been told that your smoking bothers or harms someone else?

Do you sometimes feel like a social outcast? Do you find yourself limiting your friendships to other smokers? What has your smoking meant to you personally? How has it affected your lifestyle?

Write down all the negative associations with smoking you can think of. To start you off, I'll suggest a few.

Negative Effects of Smoking

1. It makes my breath smell bad.
2. It makes me cough a lot.
3. I have to go outside to smoke; it makes me feel like an outsider.
4. Smoking makes me feel like I'm not in control of myself.
5. Smoking is not pretty or feminine.

6. I hate the dirty ashtrays and my smelly car.
7. My husband/lover doesn't want to kiss me *passionately*.
8. Cigarettes cause yellow stains on my fingers.
9. Smoking dries out my skin and makes me look older.
10. I've burned holes in some of my favorite clothes.

Now make *your* list. Write down as many as you can. Dig into your memory to recall negative associations with your smoking. The more painful incidents you can link with smoking, the better. And when you finish this list, ask yourself again, "Do I really enjoy smoking?"

Chapter 6

Your List of Negative Associations with Smoking:

1. _____
2. _____
3. _____
4. _____
5. _____
6. _____
7. _____
8. _____
9. _____
10. _____

Chapter 7

Replace Your Addiction With Something Better

If you've taken something away from yourself, your unconscious mind, like a child, needs something to replace it. It will cry out for whatever if felt has comforted it in the past—its teddy bear, pacifier or *cigarettes.* That child in you (the unreasoning part of your mind) will beg, scream and throw a tantrum. Don't give in to it. Do, however, treat it lovingly and help it find something pleasurable to do to distract it from its nagging cravings.

When we are addicted, we are not ourselves. It feels like something else, something foreign to us, has taken over our thinking. We may know that what we are doing is harmful to us, yet we cannot resist. One of the best descriptions of this process was made by the smoker who said "cigarettes boss me around."

I can recall digging in the trash to retrieve butts when I'd run out of cigarettes. I've known mothers who would leave their babies alone while they rushed out into a cold, rainy night to buy a pack.

Take back your "Self"

When we finally overcome our addiction, we take back our "Self." We are no longer driven by this destructive craving that makes us do unreasonable things. Once we convince ourselves that it is ludicrous to believe that we *enjoy* doing something that is destined to make us ill or even kill us, we are on our way to taking charge of our lives again.

So many people who have stopped smoking have found a whole new life for themselves. Often, just to take their minds off of cigarettes, they have learned a new hobby, started an exercise program or simply begun to consciously breathe differently. Any one of these things can bring about a dramatic difference in your life. In fact, this could very well be the most rewarding period of your life.

I felt that I came to life after I quit smoking. Some incredible changes came over me. As a smoker, I had always become tired and sleepy around four o'clock in the afternoon. If I could have found the time and a place, I would have taken a nap. Within two or three months of quitting, I noticed a great increase in my energy level. My afternoon tiredness and sleepiness disappeared, and I became more active than I had ever been. I doubled the laps I could swim in the pool, and along with the increased exercise came broader shoulders and a better-looking body.

When you first quit smoking, get in touch with what it was about smoking that appealed to you. For many people it's the comfort of having something in their hand, something to hold on to. For others it is oral; they like the feel of the cigarette in their mouth. Sometimes it is the feel of the smoke going into their lungs or a certain odd pleasure in watching the smoke as they blow it out. For me, like most of us, it was all of these.

At a party, it gave me something to do if I felt uncomfortable in surroundings where I knew few people. It did make it hard, though, to juggle a cigarette, a drink and food. There was always a lot of fumbling, especially if I was introduced to someone and had to find a way to shake hands.

I recall feeling so much freer after I quit. Without having the crutch of a cigarette to light and smoke, I had to find a way to overcome my shyness, and I actually became more outgoing. Sometimes people smoke to put up a "smoke screen" between themselves and others. It's interesting how much a person's personality can change when the smoke clears.

Whenever you give up something you once believed you enjoyed you must exchange it for something better. Whatever it is that you miss most when you stop smoking you must replace. I felt fidgety and needed to find something to do with my hands in the evening when I relaxed. During the first three months I crocheted five or six afghans. Everyone in the family got an afghan for Christmas that year whether they wanted one or not.

Find something to do with your hands

I've known people who learned to paint, to sculpt, to sew, to make jewelry or furniture, or even to build a vacation home. If you feel a need to do something with your hands, now is a great time to learn a new hobby. It might even be the start of a new career for you.

The important thing is not to let yourself feel

deprived. After all, you are not taking something away. You are actually giving yourself a gift—a gift of good health!

Associate healthy habits with great pleasure

If you want to give up smoking painlessly and forever, you must create permanent changes in your thinking. By associating smoking with negative feelings and linking not smoking with robust health and having fun, the urges will eventually die out by themselves. It takes only about two weeks for nicotine to leave your system. After that, you no longer have a physical addiction. It's all in the mind.

Our unconscious mind craves instant gratification. If you hit your thumb with a hammer but it didn't start to hurt until five minutes later, your unconscious would never associate that hammer with the pain it inflicted on your thumb. To reprogram your unconscious mind, you must *immediately* link smoking to pain and *immediately* link stopping smoking to pleasure.

If, every time you think of a cigarette, you say to yourself, "Yechh, that's disgusting," your unconscious will eventually get the message. But more than that is needed to feel good about your decision to quit. Now you must link *not smoking* to good feelings.

Each time you think of a cigarette but don't smoke one, think of something fun and exciting. Take several deep breaths and notice how much better you can breathe now. Thank yourself. Tell yourself how wonderful you are. Hug yourself and say "I love you!"

Immediately replace any thought of a cigarette with

a thought that brings you great pleasure. It might be the smile on your child's face. Perhaps it is a vacation you spent in the mountains or in Hawaii. It could be a walk in the woods or along the beach.

Put the money you save in a "piggy bank"

As soon as you even cut down, take the money you have saved by not buying cigarettes and put it into a piggy bank. For the first few months, at least, that you remain a nonsmoker, put the money you would have spent away. At some time, make a decision to take those savings and buy yourself something you want.

One woman I know started buying herself fresh flowers every week. She still does that even though it's been years since she quit smoking. Another woman had saved enough in a few months to buy herself a bicycle. The first thing I bought for myself after I quit was a bottle of my favorite perfume. The added bonus was that my sense of smell had improved so dramatically that the perfume smelled better to me than it ever had. Each time I wore the perfume I was reminded of my victory in overcoming my addiction.

Be good to yourself

You may want to reward yourself by taking someone you love out to dinner in some romantic restaurant. You might consider treating yourself to a short vacation. Giving yourself a tangible reward for quitting reinforces your resolve to remain a nonsmoker.

Every time you resist smoking a cigarette, thank yourself. Visualize yourself as becoming younger looking, healthier and more beautiful. This is not just a fantasy—you *will* get better looking. As the poisons leave your system, your skin will improve. It will be smoother, moister and have more color. The pallor will disappear. As your energy increases, you *will feel younger* and you *will be healthier*. Visualize this now and thank yourself. Reach around and pat yourself on the back. Look in the mirror and say "Good Show!"

Along with associating positive thoughts with not smoking, there are things you can do that help. Keep a cinnamon stick or a straw handy and stick it in your mouth whenever you think of putting a cigarette there. One woman I know who successfully quit smoking told me that she would take a deep breath through a straw then take the straw out of her mouth and exhale. She said it gave her pleasure and immediately stopped the craving for a cigarette. Notice I said that she "successfully quit," I did not call her a "quitter." Never call yourself a quitter. It carries too many negative connotations. Remember, *never confuse what you do with who you are.*

Another woman I knew kept a pencil in her hand or stuck behind her ear at all times. Whenever she thought of a cigarette, she'd twirl the pencil in her hand or tap its eraser on the desk or even write down a reason she was glad she wasn't smoking. It worked for her.

The urge will pass—wait it out!

The most important fact I learned after I quit smoking was that all urges pass within a short period

Chapter 7

of time. You have to deal with only a moment at a time. All you have to do when you have an urge is *wait it out!* It will soon go away. It may return later, but you can deal with it in the same way the next time.

Here's some more good news. If you quit smoking before you have developed emphysema or any other irreversible condition, your chances of eventually becoming ill or dying from the effects of smoking are *dramatically decreased*. After 8 to 10 years of not smoking, most people are as healthy as they would have been if they had never smoked at all. It is possible to recover virtually all of your lung capacity.

Another piece of good news is that you will be more relaxed when you *don't smoke*. The relaxation you experience when you smoke a cigarette only comes with the first few puffs. It is really just temporary relief from the tension caused from your body's craving for nicotine. If you had never smoked, you'd never need that fix. Smoking actually increases your blood pressure and heart rate. Although that first puff has relaxed you, as you keep smoking, you become more nervous.

There are a lot of good reasons for not smoking. You have many personal, private and painful experiences relating to smoking. Everyone does. They can range from burning a hole in their favorite dress or suit to burning down a house. Some of these stories are funny, some are tragic. But now that you know beyond a shadow of a doubt that smoking is bad for you, think of all the good things you can experience when you don't smoke. Write down all the reasons you can think of for not smoking. Here are a few examples:

Positive Benefits of Not Smoking:
1. My sense of taste will improve.
2. I'll be able to smell my roses.
3. My breath, my car and my clothes will smell better.
4. I'll be able to run farther and faster.
5. I will live a longer, healthier life.
6. It will make my lover/children/husband happy.
7. I will have more energy and enjoy life more.
8. I won't be ostracized by nonsmokers or feel like an outcast.
9. I'll look better; I'll look younger and fitter.
10. I'll be sexier. My libido will increase.

Write your list now. Be creative. Think of all of the many ways your life will improve. Write down all the reasons you want to be free from smoking and make them very personal. Then put this list on your refrigerator, on the wall next to your desk, in your purse or pocket, and look at it whenever you feel you might weaken. (You can have a different, less personal list at the office. Everyone doesn't have to know the intimate details of your life.)

Make your list of all the ways your life will improve.

1. _____
2. _____
3. _____
4. _____
5. _____
6. _____
7. _____
8. _____
9. _____
10. _____

Keep active – do something productive and fun

Now that you've made your decision to get rid of your cigarettes for good, make a list of things you are going to replace them with. It is important for you to do something new that will keep your mind and your hands active. You don't have to limit the list. But you must be sure that you will do all the things that you plan to do. These are promises to yourself. It is imperative that you keep these promises. Here are some examples:

1. I will take golf (or tennis or dancing) lessons.
2. I will learn to make jewelry.
3. I'll restore antique furniture.
4. I'll start painting (or sculpting).
5. I'll buy a camera and sign up for a photography class.

Now write down all the things you would like to do; list them in order of importance.

Write your list here.

1. _____
2. _____
3. _____
4. _____
5. _____
6. _____
7. _____
8. _____
9. _____
10. _____

Carry out your plan

The next thing to do is to begin researching how you are going to carry out your plan. Find a tennis teacher and start taking lessons. Check the classifieds for antique furniture for sale. Sign up for jewelry making or painting classes at the local college. Take action, don't just talk about it. Not only will you be taking your mind off cigarettes and keeping your hands busy, you'll be on your way to a healthier, happier, more productive and more rewarding life.

Chapter 8

Deep Breathing, Relaxation and Visualization

Perhaps the most important thing to learn to do when you are breaking the smoking habit is deep breathing. Nearly every smoker I've worked with has stated that deep breathing helped more than anything else in dealing with their sudden urges for a cigarette. Taking deep breaths is something you can do anytime and anywhere.

Smokers tend to have shallow breathing. The only time they take a deep breath is when they are taking a drag on a cigarette and pulling the smoke into their lungs. Yet, breathing is one of our most important bodily functions. We can go without food for weeks and without water for days, but if we go without oxygen for even a few minutes, we can suffer irreversible brain damage or death.

Our bodies are rhythmically joined with the planet in a continual exchange of matter and energy. One way this exchange occurs is through breathing. Carbon dioxide molecules from inside our bodies are exchanged for oxygen molecules from the air around us each time we breathe in and out. Our bodies dispose of waste products each time we exhale and become renewed each time we inhale.

An important partner in this process is the heart. During our entire lifetime it never stops pumping. It beats day in and day out, year in and year out without a rest for all the years of our lives. It pumps oxygen-rich blood from our lungs through our arteries and capillaries to every cell in our body. Our red blood cells exchange their oxygen for the major waste product of all living tissue, carbon dioxide, and carry this waste product back to the heart which pumps it to the lungs. The lungs then discharge it into the atmosphere through exhaling.

Proper breathing plays an important role in healing, in relaxation, in meditation and in controlling our emotions. Breathing exercises are used in labor and childbirth to ease the pain; in psychotherapy to help a troubled person get in touch with her feelings; in medicine to assist in the healing process and in spiritual quests to help the seeker reach a higher level of consciousness. Deep breathing is invaluable in the process of overcoming addictions.

In his book *The Healing Heart*, Norman Cousins explains the role of deep, regular breathing in the relaxation response techniques developed by his cardiologist, Dr. Herbert Bensen. The techniques, which he compared to transcendental meditation or self-hypnosis, brought about striking results. Norman Cousins' heart attack was extremely serious, but he recovered, due, in large part, to the noninvasive, natural treatments he received that included deep breathing exercises. Other patients with heart disorders have also experienced great improvement in their condition, including significant reductions in the fatty content of their blood.

Gloria Steinem, in her best-selling book on self-esteem, *Revolution From Within*, states, "The way we breathe can influence our state of mind." She goes on to explain that "because it is the one autonomic process that can easily be regulated, it can and should be a bridge to exploring many of our untapped powers." Exhaling slowly can calm the mind and inhaling more slowly than we exhale can energize it.

In his Stress Reduction Clinic at the University of Massachusetts Medical Center, Dr. Jon Kabat-Zinn teaches "mindful breathing," a method of tuning in to our breathing to help calm the mind and the body. He believes that by being aware of our thoughts and feelings with a greater degree of calmness, we are able to see things more clearly and with a larger perspective.

Practice deep-breathing exercises regularly

There are many different kinds of breathing exercises, but for our purposes I would like to present a couple of very simple ones. The major benefits as they are presented here are relaxation and healing. The first one was shown to me many years ago by my voice teacher, and its purpose was to increase my lung capacity so that I would have greater control over my breath and voice. This is the one I usually use in my smoking-cessation program:

- Breathe in slowly to the count of ten.
- Hold your breath for the count of five.
- Breath out slowly to the count of ten. Make sure you push all of your breath out of your lungs.
- Hold your breath for the count of five.
- Repeat the exercise ten times while reclining, if possible.

At first you may wish to count to ten within a period of five seconds and hold your breath for two or three seconds. As you increase your lung capacity, you should count slower and breathe more deeply. According to my teacher, doing the deep-breathing exercise in this manner prevents you from hyperventilating and getting dizzy. Even if that is so, I do not recommend doing this breathing exercise while driving.

Another breathing exercise you can do is to breathe in while holding your fingers on your pulse. This coordinates the rhythm of your heartbeat with the rhythm of your breathing. In this exercise, I breathe in to the count of eight heartbeats; I hold my breath for only two heartbeats, then breathe out for the count of ten, holding my breath for two heartbeats.

For situations where you cannot lie down or sit quietly in a chair to do your breathing exercises, practice a shorter, milder version of either of the above.

Pay attention to your breath
Once you feel comfortable with either of the two breathing exercises, you can start paying attention to how your breath feels going in and out and what is happening to your body as you breathe.

When you breathe in, your abdomen should rise. Be careful not to raise your shoulders. The breath should be pulled deep inside your lungs, all the way to the bottom of them, expanding them to the fullest possible extent. As you exhale, pull your abdomen in, pushing all the air out of your lungs that you can. This, by the way, also helps exercise your abdominal muscles, giving you a flatter-looking tummy.

Do not let your mind wander. Keep it focused on the process at hand. If you find yourself thinking of other things, bring yourself back to your breathing. How does the air feel as it enters your mouth and proceeds down your air passage into your lungs? As you exhale, concentrate on how it feels as it leaves your body. Visualize yourself breathing in good, cleansing, healthy air and breathing out any toxins that may have accumulated in your body.

At first you may find yourself coughing as you do this exercise, especially if you are a heavy smoker. This is a good sign. This means that your body is trying to rid itself of the smoke and toxic substances that remain in your lungs from smoking. Let yourself cough, don't suppress it. Take a drink of water if you need to, then resume your breathing exercises.

After awhile, when you are no longer smoking and have increased your lung capacity, you will be able to do the breathing exercises without coughing. When you have completed the exercise, you will find that your body and your mind have become calmer.

A "touchstone"

In my stop-smoking classes, I give each participant one of the small, smooth, round stones that I pick up during my walks on the beach. There are several reasons for this, but the main one is that I have found that holding the stone loosely in the hand seems to help calm the mind.

I first discovered this a few years ago when I was working a job that paid very well but which I disliked. Every morning, to prepare myself for the day, I would walk along the beach. One morning, I was particularly unhappy about going to this job that was so unsuitable for me. I was trying to decide whether to quit and pursue my dream, which was writing full time, or to do the "sensible" thing and stay on this job while I looked for another job that was more suitable.

While I was walking slowly on the beach, deep in thought and staring down blankly at the sand, I saw a shiny, blood-red stone and picked it up. It fit into the palm of my hand perfectly, and I closed my fingers around it. As it warmed up in my hand, I began to feel more peaceful, and by the time it was the temperature of my hand, I was feeling quite calm. As I became calm, my thinking seemed to clear, and I resolved right then to trust my own ingenuity and talents and put all my efforts into writing. That day I gave my notice.

Since then, I will pick up that stone whenever I find myself worrying about my future, uncertain about a decision in my life or feeling stressed for any reason. I have discovered that the intensity of such feelings have a limited time span. That time span seems to coincide closely with the time it takes the small stone to warm to the temperature of my hand. It isn't that the worries go away, it's just that I am able to put them into the proper perspective when I take a few moments to let myself be calm and clear my mind.

After you have quit smoking, there may be times, now and then, when you feel nearly overcome with the craving for a cigarette. The greatest intensity of that craving only lasts a short while—usually only a minute or two. That is what I noticed when I quit smoking for good. I found that if I could just "wait it out" the craving would go away. I didn't allow myself to think beyond those next few minutes. All I had to do was get through that period. I would deal with the next wave of desire when, and if, it came. This philosophy is similar to the "one day at a time" credo of Alcoholics Anonymous. And it works!

When I use this stone in the stop-smoking program, I call it a "touchstone." The dictionary defines touchstone as "a test or criterion for the qualities of a thing." You can use it to test the quality and duration of your urges. If you hold it in your hand when you have an urge for a cigarette, you will notice that the urge will pass in about the same amount of time it takes for the stone to warm up. In that way the stone can work as a timer—and a reminder.

Another advantage is that the stone gives you something tangible to "hold on to." As part of the appeal of cigarettes is tactile, the stone is a substitute for the feel of a cigarette in your hand. If you make positive associations with the stone, it can help to keep you grounded. If you can find a metaphysical use for it, all the better.

The stones I choose fit well into the palm of most people's hand with their fingers closed around it. They are very smooth, round, sea-tossed, nonporous stones, like marble. They feel better in the hand and they take longer to warm up than a porous one would. If you don't have access to beach stones, find any small object that fits into the palm of your hand. It could be a large marble or metal ball. Hold it loosely in your hand when you do your relaxation exercises. Afterward, whenever you hold that object in your hand, your subconscious mind is reminded to relax.

Once you have oxygenated your lungs and have allowed yourself to feel calm, you can begin to practice relaxation and visualization. The following are a couple of suggested exercises. You may wish to choose one to do regularly or you might want to alternate them.

Relaxation Exercise #1:

Imagine yourself standing beside a hot tub. There are small bubbles coming from the bottom of the tub and slowly floating to the top. You can see steam rising from the surface of the water. As you dip your right foot into it, you notice that it is slightly warmer than body temperature. You step down onto the first step. The water is just above your ankle. Then you step down with the other foot. You take another step down with your right foot, then with your left. The water is now up to your knees. You notice a soft, warm massage from the swirling bubbly water, and your body begins to feel warmer. Two more steps down and the warm water is mid-thigh. Now you sit down on a step and feel the water as it comes up to your waist. Scooting down another couple of steps, you are now sitting deep in the water and feel it warming your entire body. Only your head is out of the water, and you feel the relaxation created by the soft, bubbly water seeping into every muscle and cell of your body. You are now peaceful, calm and comfortable.

Relaxation Exercise #2:

Lie on your back on your bed, a couch or the floor. Let your arms lay by your side, your feet slightly apart. Now starting with your toes, tense them as though you were clinching your fists. Relax them. Next, pull your toes up toward your ankles and relax them. Tense the muscles in your calves and relax them. Then tense the muscles in your thighs and relax. Tighten your hips and relax. Pull in your stomach muscles and relax. Now lift and tighten your shoulders. Relax them. Clinch your fists and relax. Tense the muscles in both arms and relax. Tighten your neck muscles and relax. Tighten all the muscles in your face and relax. Now tense all of the muscles together in your entire body and hold the tension tightly for five seconds. Relax. Your body is now completely relaxed. Let it sink into the bed. Feel all the tension slip away. Take a long,

*satisfying, deep breath, then exhale. You now feel
calm, relaxed, warm and comfortable.*

The above exercises should take from five to ten minutes. If you take longer, all the better. Once you are feeling relaxed you are ready for visualization. Keep your mind clear. Do not let it wander to anything in the past or to any thoughts or concerns for the future. Keep your thoughts in the moment.

What you visualize should be what is dear to you. Choose a setting, a season, a view that you enjoy. Place yourself in that setting. It may be a place you have been before where you felt at peace. Let yourself feel the air on your skin, the sound of the sand or forest floor under your feet and the rustle of the wind in the trees. Recall the sunset over the ocean, the rainbow in the mountains, the smell of pine trees, flowers or sagebrush in the air...

Here are some suggested exercises.

Visualization Exercise #1:

You are in the forest in the mountains. You have on comfortable shoes and are dressed in warm, loose clothing. As you walk along a path, you notice that the wild irises are in bloom and new, pale green leaves are emerging from the dry, brown branches of the trees. Tall redwoods cast lacy shadows across the path and you can smell the pungent scent of pine and cedar in the air. With each step you can hear the crunch of your shoe meeting the soft ground cushioned by years of falling leaves, pine needles

Chapter 8

and small twigs. You look up and see golden eagles soaring like magical kites in the sky above. Dainty, red-throated hummingbirds hover in front of blue trumpet-shaped flowers on a vine wound around an old rough-hewn wooden fence. In the distance you can hear the howl of a coyote, the chattering of tree squirrels, the tap-tap-tapping of a woodpecker. A young deer steps onto the path in front of you, stops briefly and stares, then moves on slowly, disappearing into the thick woods. The spring air is cool and crisp, but you are comfortable and warm.

After awhile, you come upon a clearing in the woods. It is a high meadow carpeted with wildflowers of every kind and color. At the other side of it you see an inviting log lying on the ground. You walk to it and sit down to rest. You discover that you are on the ridge of the mountain and, looking down, you can see miles and miles of desert stretching out below. A warm breeze reaches up to you from the desert floor bringing with it the perfume of cactus flowers and sagebrush. You feel rested and peaceful. The only sounds you hear are the wind through the pine needles, a chorus of birds and the harmonious whisperings of the wilderness. The air is clearer, purer and sweeter than you have ever known it to be, and you take several deliciously deep breaths.

You glance at the ground by your feet and see a pack of cigarettes. It's your brand. You pick them up, open the pack and reach in for a cigarette. Suddenly the cigarettes turn into crawling, slimy worms which start to slither up onto your hands.

As they touch your skin they burn and itch. You drop the package and stand up, frantically brushing off the worms. Finally, you get them all off and feel a sense of relief. You get a stick and dig a hole, then with the stick you push the pack of cigarettes into it and cover it up.

You are now calm again, but it's starting to get dark and the weather has turned colder. You start for home. A short distance away you can see your small, cozy cabin and you walk toward it. You enter, build a fire in the fireplace and sit in front of it with a warm cup of cocoa or tea. You realize how wonderfully healthy you feel now that you have broken the spell of cigarettes. You take another deep breath and relax deeply into the sofa.

Visualization Exercise #2:

You are walking along the beach. No other person is on the beach but you. The sky is clear with only some wispy clouds drifting lazily along the horizon. It is warm and you can feel the sun on your body and a balmy breeze softly ruffling your hair. The ocean is calm and the waves wash up languidly onto the beach and slowly recede. You can hear the rhythmic whisper of the surf. You are feeling freer, calmer and happier than you can ever remember. You take a deep breath and feel clean, fresh air enter your lungs. You are reminded that you once smoked but that you no longer do. As you breathe clearly and easily you thank yourself for the great gift of health that you have given yourself.

Chapter 8 / 2 /

You know that this is the way you always want to breathe. You are aware of the fresh air going in and out of your body. With each breath, you can feel your lungs clearing up. You can feel the waste materials of the past exiting your body. Your lungs feel stronger and healthier with every breath you take...

You see someone walking toward you now on the beach, carrying a cigarette. As he (or she) approaches you, he hands you a long, freshly lighted cigarette. Immediately, the smoke blows into your face and burns your eyes and the smell of it makes you feel slightly nauseous. You take the cigarette in your hand and look at it. It feels hot and it irritates your hand. When you put it to your mouth, it tastes bitter and rotten. As you watch, it suddenly turns into an ugly, poisonous bug which tries to bite you. Quickly you heave it as far as you can into the ocean. A wave catches it, tears it apart and takes it out to sea. You feel relieved, safe again. You feel thankful that you are now free of the poison you once put into your body.

You continue on your walk. The person with the cigarette has disappeared and you are once again alone. You regain your sense of peace, good health and happiness.

From now on, every time you think of smoking a cigarette, you can remember how good it feels to breathe clean, fresh air. You can recall how poisonous the cigarette is, how bad it tastes and smells and you can be grateful that you no longer smoke. Thank yourself that you have given up cigarettes forever. Whenever you see other people smoking, visualize yourself in that beautiful place where you breathe clean air. In this special place you have overcome an illness and are healthy once more. Having overcome this obstacle, you realize that you can take on any challenge in your life and be successful.

Enjoying the tranquillity of your feelings and the abundant energy that you now have you may allow yourself to come back into your present environment. Notice yourself in your bed (or on the floor or couch) and feel free and happy that you have regained control of yourself, your health and your life. Allow yourself to feel that you have received a reward, a gift and an honor—and that you richly deserve it.

You may use this visualization exercise as it is, alter it to suit you or devise one of your own. Whichever you decide to do, write it out, then record it on an audiocassette tape in your own voice. Each morning or night (both if you have the time) lie down in a quiet place, do your deep breathing exercises, turn on your tape recorder and play it back to yourself. Twenty minutes, twice a day is the optimal amount of time to spend for best results. But even if it is only five or ten minutes that you spend at each session, you will benefit.

You may call it visualization, imaging, autosuggestion, self-hypnosis or daydreaming. But, whatever you call it, it works.

You will soon find that a cigarette doesn't have the same hold on you. It doesn't have the same appeal anymore. What becomes more appealing to you is to have sound, clear lungs, more energy and greater control over your life.

The deep breathing and relaxation exercises alone will help relieve your stress. Stress plays a major role in sustaining any undesirable habit or addiction. When we feel stressed, it seems that something or someone else is in charge of us. Something other than our own true selves dictates how we will react in uncomfortable situations. We are not running our lives, our lives are running us.

When we feel stressed we are often compelled to do things that are not in our own best interest. We become like a leaf blowing in the wind. Where we go and how we end up is out of our control. We are at the mercy of every ill wind that drifts into our path.

Once we have become addicted to nicotine, we become stressed if that "fix" is denied us. As explained earlier, the first puff or two satisfies the cravings, then the stimulant quality of cigarettes increases our heart rate and makes us feel even more stressed. It becomes a vicious cycle. When we learn to relieve our stress in healthier ways, we will no longer need to smoke.

Stress reduction

The first thing we must take care of, then, is our stress level. Although what happens in our lives is often out of our control, our *reaction* to what happens is not. By calming yourself down through deep breathing and relaxation exercises, you will be able to reduce your stress. Practiced regularly, these simple techniques can help you regain control of your emotions.

When you add visualization to your stress reduction program, you can eliminate the appeal that smoking has had for you. Not only that, you can change your life in wonderful and amazing ways.

Chapter 9

Exercise and the Nonsmoking Diet

There are many good reasons to exercise and to eat the right foods, but the reason that is at the top of most women's list is *weight*. You have heard the horror stories of women who quit smoking and immediately gained 20 or 30 pounds. Actually, there often is some weight gain, but the average gain is only 5 to 8 pounds.

Smokers tend to wrinkle early. If I had to make a choice between quitting smoking and gaining weight or continuing to smoke and getting wrinkles, it would be to quit smoking. You can take the weight off again but once you get wrinkles they are there to stay. The only thing you can do about those extra lines in your face is get a face-lift.

There are several reasons that some women gain weight when they quit smoking. Among those reasons are the following:

1. Food may be used as a substitute for a cigarette. Ex-smokers may substitute a cigarette with a candy bar or some other high-caloric food.

2. Food may be used as a reward. Where once they smoked a cigarette after a particular chore, former smokers sometimes reward themselves with a snack.

3. Food often tastes better. As taste buds come alive again, eating becomes more enjoyable and it's tempting to eat more.

4. Some researchers believe that, as nicotine increases the heart rate, it may also increase the metabolic rate and actually burn food faster. That is the reason many women believe that smoking keeps their weight down.

Just because some people gain weight when they quit smoking doesn't mean that *you* have to. There are many things you can do to avoid that undesirable side effect. You actually can eat more than you did when you were a smoker and not gain weight, but you must eat *differently*. It is important, in fact, imperative, that you eat more *often* than you did before. Instead of three large meals each day, it is recommended that you eat six small ones a day. You can spread the same amount of calories out over the course of the day by eating smaller portions every two or three hours.

People with diabetes, hypoglycemia and other medical problems have to do this. But it's really the best way to eat for anyone. When we eat more often our body operates more efficiently and burns more calories. It has been shown that people can actually lose weight eating the same amount of calories if they spread out the calories into six or seven portions each day. Researchers have also found that by eating most of your calories early in the day you burn them faster and more efficiently. Most of the very slender people I know don't even eat a full dinner. They have only a light snack in the evening.

We feel stressed when our stomach gets empty. As nicotine suppresses the appetite in some people, you may experience a greater sense of hunger when you quit smoking. Eating every two or three hours keeps the stomach full so that you don't get hungry. It also reduces the temptation to eat too much and to eat the wrong things.

As mentioned in a previous chapter, there are certain foods to avoid during the one to two weeks before your menstrual period. These are high calcium foods such as dairy products, green leafy vegetables, caffeinated beverages, white bread and alcohol. (See list of foods in Chapter Two.)

Keep snacks handy

It's a good idea to carry snacks with you wherever you go to nibble on when you get hungry or just want to put something into your mouth (instead of a cigarette). If you are not in that "down" part of your premenstrual phase, these snacks can be low-calorie, crunchy foods such as celery, jicama and carrot sticks.

If you are in your PMS phase, the snacks you should have include raw, fresh mushrooms, green peas and bell pepper. All of these foods are low in calories.

Green peas may have more calories than the others, but they aren't nearly as high as candy or other sweets. These foods will stay fresh and crispy if you carry them in a plastic bag inside a small paper bag and they should fit in your briefcase or purse quite easily.

Pine nuts, pumpkin seeds, sesame seeds, walnuts, peanuts and cashews are all high in magnesium, so they are okay to eat at any time during your cycle. They are also very easy to carry as they don't spoil and they take up very little room. If you crave sweets, you might want to put a few raisins in the baggie along with the seeds and nuts. But all of these are high in calories. Consult a calorie chart and limit your consumption of these accordingly.

By including the above foods in your diet each day and by eating regularly and often, you will be accomplishing several goals. You will reduce stress, hunger pangs and the temptation to smoke. If you become aware of how many calories you are consuming each day, you will also reduce the likelihood of gaining weight.

A rule of thumb for keeping your weight down is to consume about a hundred calories for each pound of body weight each day. For instance, if you weigh 140 pounds, you should eat no more than 1,400 calories a day. If you are exercising regularly, you can have more calories.

One way of keeping your calories down is to reduce the fats in your diet. If you usually take cream in your coffee, use nonfat milk instead, or drink it black. Use low-calorie mayonnaise or substitute mustard on your sandwiches. Use low-fat salad dressing or squeeze fresh lemon juice onto your salads. Unless you have a problem with salt, you can use soy sauce on your meats and vegetables in place of butter. There is also low-salt soy sauce and I can't tell the difference. I sometimes dip my steamed vegetables in Dijon mustard and it's quite tasty. When I want to give myself a treat, I'll have a small dish of nonfat frozen yogurt. It's delicious and very low in calories.

The need for extra nutrients or supplements

Smokers' nutritional requirements are different from nonsmokers'. Nicotine robs the body of vitamin C and increases the need for antioxidants. Smoking depletes the body's store of B vitamins. Until your body returns to normal, it would be wise to supplement your diet with foods high in these properties or even to take vitamin supplements.

I started taking vitamin supplements as I was cutting down on my smoking and have continued because they seem to work for me. I believe, along with Dr. Linus Pauling and many other researchers, that vitamins C and E and beta carotene are very beneficial in helping guard against illness. Since I quit smoking I rarely get a cold or the flu or, for that matter, anything else. I don't attribute my excellent health to stopping smoking alone, although that had a great deal to do with it. I also take 2,000 units of vitamin C, 400 units of vitamin E and 25,000 units of beta carotene every day. I have recently added magnesium to my arsenal. I do not take a multivitamin since I eat a very well-balanced diet. The PMS diet presented here is recommended by the Lawrences, mentioned before in Chapter Two. Dr. Allen Lawrence is a gynecologist and his wife, Lisa, is a nutritionist. Between them they have written many books on health and natural healing and have been very generous in advising me on the nonsmoking diet for women. They advise their smoking patients to take a B complex which includes at least 300 units of B_6. They also suggest a magnesium supplement which contains 250 to 500 mg of magnesium. These are also particularly helpful for the PMS woman.

Living in a city exposes us to many pollutants, and these supplements help protect us from them. Again, this is a matter of personal belief and the choice of whether to take supplements is yours to make. Before you go out and buy a bunch of vitamins, you should check with your doctor. As I am not a medical doctor, I don't wish to prescribe anything other than good, fresh, healthy food to help you get through the next few weeks and months.

You might find, once you begin eating a healthier diet, that you feel so much better you will want to continue eating this way the rest of your life. I hope you do.

If you eat out most of the time, take the list of recommended foods with you to refer to in your choices. If you cook often, you might want to try some of the following original recipes for meals and snacks that are nutritious, low in calories and/or fats and suitable for the PMS woman. I have included them to show that it is possible to meet all the above criteria and still eat delicious foods. These have been taste-tested by my friends, family and myself, and I believe you'll find that not only will you enjoy them, but others you cook for will like them, too.

🌺 HOPPIN' JOHN

This is an old Arkansas recipe that I modified to reduce the fat and calories. The original contained white instead of brown rice and salt pork in place of the turkey sausage. I also make this as a soup simply by adding more water and more seasonings.

> 1 cup dried black-eyed peas
> dash of Tabasco sauce
> 3 cups water
> 1 teaspoon salt
> 1 medium-size onion, diced
> ½ teaspoon crushed pepper
> ½ cup brown rice
> 1 teaspoon Worcestershire sauce
> ½ pound low-fat turkey sausage

Wash peas and pick over carefully. Place in large pot and cover with 3 cups of water. Bring to a boil and cook for a minute or two. Turn off heat and let stand for an hour. Drain and rinse (if desired). Add 3 cups of water, onion, salt, pepper, Tabasco and Worcestershire sauce and again bring to a boil. Lower heat and simmer for one hour. Add brown rice and diced turkey sausage and more water, if necessary. Simmer one hour or until done. (One serving = about 150 calories.) Serve with hot cornbread and a salad for a well-balanced meal. Serves eight.

🌸 SAN BUENAVENTURA GUACAMOLE
1 cup mashed ripe avocados
1 tablespoon finely grated onions
2 tablespoons fresh lemon juice
½ teaspoon garlic powder
¼ teaspoon chili powder
salt to taste
4 corn tortillas

Mix avocados with onions, lemon juice, garlic powder, chili powder and salt. To make tortilla chips, cut tortillas in eighths and bake in a 400 degree oven until they brown lightly and curl. Dip tortilla chips into guacamole. (One serving = 135 calories) Serves four.

🌸 HAWAIIAN TOFU STIR-FRY
This vegetarian dish can be made with chicken cubes or ground beef instead of walnuts for about the same amount of calories.

4 oz. firm tofu, rinsed, drained and blotted dry
1 small onion
1 oz. candied ginger, chopped fine
1 egg
1 cup bean sprouts

⅓ cup vegetable broth
½ cup walnuts
2 tablespoons soy sauce
2 cups hot cooked brown rice
½ lb. fresh mushrooms, sliced
1 tablespoon sliced green onions

Cut tofu into ½-inch cubes. Beat together egg, water and soy sauce in a separate bowl at set aside. Heat peanut oil in wok until hot. Then add mushrooms, onion, walnuts and stir-fry until lightly browned. Stir in tofu cubes and ginger; sprinkle with water. Stir-fry 30 seconds; cover and steam for one minute. Stir in bean sprouts and egg mixture and stir-fry for another minute. Serve over rice and garnish with green onion. (One serving = about 310 calories) Serves four.

🏵 LINGUINI AND CLAM SAUCE
4 small cans chopped clams
1 lg. can chopped Italian tomatoes
1 med. onion
¼ cup chopped fresh parsley
3 cloves garlic
¼ cup chopped fresh cilantro
½ cup chopped celery
dried oregano and basil
2 tablespoons olive oil
1 pkg. linguini

Sauté onion, garlic and celery in olive oil until lightly browned. Add tomatoes, oregano and basil and simmer for ten minutes. Drain clams, reserving ¼ cup of the liquid. Add clams, liquid, parsley and cilantro. Simmer for five to ten minutes. Serve sauce over hot, cooked linguini. (One serving = 210 calories) Serves six or more.

You may wish to sprinkle grated parmesan or Romano cheese on top, but it is not necessary as it is very tasty without the cheese. I usually serve this with whole wheat bread sticks and a tossed green salad.

❧ LEMON-HERB BAKED CHICKEN
4 medium-size chicken breasts
¼ cup fresh lemon juice
dried basil, oregano and parsley
3 large cloves fresh garlic
salt and pepper to taste
fresh cilantro

Preheat oven to 350 degrees. Skin chicken breasts, rinse and dry. Rub on olive oil and place meaty side down in baking pan. Sprinkle with herbs, salt and pepper. Turn over, pour half of lemon juice over them and sprinkle with herbs, salt and pepper. Put garlic through garlic press and spread on top of chicken. Bake 30 to 40 minutes, turning and basting with lemon juice twice. Remove to platter. Stir two tablespoons of lemon juice and about ¼ cup of chicken broth in same baking pan the chicken was baked in, scraping the bottom of the pan and simmer until the liquid reduces slightly. Spoon the sauce over the chicken. Garnish with fresh cilantro. (One serving = about 140 calories) Serves four.

You might want to serve this dish with the following:

🌿 VEGETABLE AND RICE STIR-FRY
½ lb. fresh mushrooms, sliced
1 (16 oz.) can Italian tomatoes
1 large onion
1 teaspoon dried oregano
1 green bell pepper
¼ teaspoon salt
¼ lb. fresh green beans
½ cup frozen whole-kernel corn
3 cups cooked brown rice

Sauté mushrooms, onion, green pepper and green beans in peanut oil for one minute. Cover and steam one minute. Crush tomatoes and add along with juice, oregano and salt. Simmer until reduced by half. Stir in corn and rice and stir until heated through. (One serving = 210 calories) Serves four.

The following recipe is very low in calories but not necessarily suitable if you are in your PMS phase.

🌸 CONFETTI SLAW
2 cups shredded white cabbage
Juice of one lemon
1 cup shredded red cabbage
1 T. low-calorie mayonnaise
½ cup shredded carrots
1 tsp. dark sesame oil
¼ tsp. garlic powder
salt and pepper to taste

Toss cabbage and carrots together lightly. Mix together lemon, mayonnaise, sesame oil and garlic powder in separate bowl. Combine with cabbage and carrots and toss lightly. Add salt and pepper to taste. (One serving = 20 calories) Makes six servings. I often add ⅛ -cup of sunflower seeds to this recipe for extra flavor and nutrition and it's delicious, but then it adds up to 45 calories per serving.

For dessert you can have a dish of fresh-sliced bananas and passion fruit. If you are not concerned with PMS, you may add diced apples, pineapple and oranges. A great topping for this is a creamy mixture of low-fat or non-fat sour cream seasoned with a teaspoon of almond extract and a little raw sugar. Mix this together at least an hour before serving and refrigerate. When you get ready to serve, stir thoroughly and place a small dollop on top of each dish of fresh fruit. The number of calories you end up with depends on the kinds of fruits and sour cream you use.

Remember, you can eat potatoes at any time

during your cycle and a baked potato contains less than 100 calories. Just be careful of the topping. That is usually where all the calories come from.

Soups and salads are almost always good to eat to keep your weight down, as long as you don't eat a lot of creamed soups and don't use high-calorie dressings on your salad. Both of these are light and usually have a good deal of water in ratio to the solids, so they move quickly through your system. There are also some very tasty crackers on the market now that are low in fat and calories. You can even buy potato chips that have been baked instead of fried.

Chicken, turkey and fish are all high in magnesium and B_6. Remember to take the skin off of the chicken and turkey, as they add to the fat content.

Cooking destroys vitamin B_6 so it's important not to boil food. Steaming is usually best as more vitamins are retained that way. When you cook rice, for example, bring the water to a boil, then let it cool a few seconds before adding the rice. Cook on a very low simmer. Again, steaming is better than cooking in water.

Corn on the cob should never be cooked longer than two or three minutes. One excellent way to cook it is to clean it and rewrap in the husk, then to place it in a microwave for a minute or two. It cooks in its own natural package and retains the flavor and nutritive value.

During these first few weeks when you are overcoming your urges to smoke, food can be a friend. There is certainly nothing wrong with turning your focus onto food. Your taste buds will be sharper and you will probably enjoy food more than you have in a very long time. You can discover a new adventure in eating by finding delicious low-fat, low-calorie recipes to prepare and restaurants that serve fresh, nutritious and healthful foods. You may learn a whole new way of eating that will enhance your health and energy level for all of your life, not just now.

The above recipes are just examples of a few flavorful dishes you can eat and still stay with the program. Using the list of recommended foods, you will be able to devise your own. It's a good idea to put all the recipes you love on 3 x 5 cards and keep a file of them. You could start a recipe exchange club with other women who have PMS, a weight problem, who are quitting smoking or who simply want to be healthier.

Probably as important as diet at this time is exercise.

Exercise regularly

Exercise not only can help you keep your weight down, it can also help you overcome stress and take your mind off of cigarettes. If you had considered taking up some sport as a hobby such as tennis or swimming, now is the time to do it. Taking lessons will help you get into the sport and enjoy it more. You might want to buy some exercise equipment or join a gym with the money you save by not smoking but this isn't necessary.

Walking is an excellent exercise and it requires no outlay of money, except maybe for a good, comfortable pair of walking shoes. Along with walking, you should do some stretching exercises every day. If you only can spend a half-hour a day exercising, ten minutes should be spent stretching and twenty minutes in walking.

Here are a few stretching exercises that will help you stay limber and also help you avoid back problems as well as relieve back pain. Most smokers are not as energetic nor as active physically as nonsmokers are. Certainly, they aren't as active as they would be if they didn't smoke. For this reason as well as, perhaps, many other reasons, most smokers suffer with back pain. These exercises will definitely help. They are simple, mild and easy to do.

One caution, though, before you begin any exercise regime, it's best to check with your doctor to see if they are appropriate for you.

Floor exercises:

❦ Lying flat on your back with your arms stretched out to the side, pull your right knee up toward your chest. Place your left hand on your knee and pull it toward the floor on the left side, keeping your shoulders on the floor. Touch the floor with your right knee if you can. Hold it for a few seconds, then reverse legs and repeat with your left knee. Do this exercise three to five times.

❦ Still lying on your back, bend your right knee with your foot on the floor, then lift and lower your left leg slowly 10 times, not letting your heel touch the floor. Repeat with your other leg.

❧ Bending both knees, place your hands behind your head and lift your shoulders from the floor. Lift your left knee, twist your upper body to the right and touch your left knee with your right elbow. Then lift your right knee and touch it with your left elbow. Repeat ten times.

❧ Lying on your left side, bend your left knee and lift your right leg as high as you can toward the ceiling. Lower it slowly, not touching the floor and raise it again. Repeat 10 times and reverse.

❧ Sit up and bend your knees, touching the soles of your feet together, knees on the floor. Stretch your arms out in front of you and bend your upper body as far as you can slowly toward the floor, keeping your back straight. Resume sitting position and repeat 10 times.

❧ Sitting on the floor with your back straight, stretch your legs as far apart as possible. Bend to the left slowly and touch your left ankle with both hands. Resume sitting position and bend to the right, touching your right ankle. Repeat 10 times.

❧ Getting on your hands and knees, lift your back as far as you can from the floor, then lower it as close as you can to the floor. Repeat 10 times.

Standing exercises

🌺 Stand up and stretch your arms straight out to the side. Without turning your hips, twist your body above your waist as far as you can to one side and then to the other. Look directly in back of you as you do this. Repeat 10 times.

🌺 Place your left hand on your waist and raise your right arm as high as you can toward the ceiling. Bend to the left without moving your hips, and stretch as far as you can. Then bend toward the eleven o'clock position, and with your arm parallel to the floor, stretch and hold it for five seconds. Let your arm move to center front and point toward the ground. Bring your left arm down beside it and slowly raise your body to a standing position again. Repeat on other side.

🌺 With left hand on hip, rotate right arm as though you are swimming a backstroke ten times; then rotate it in the opposite direction. Place right hand on hip and repeat with left arm.

🌺 Turn head as far as you can to the right and look behind you, hold for five seconds, then to the left and hold for five seconds. Repeat three times.

🌺 Lift both shoulders and rotate from front to back five times. Then rotate from back to front five times.

These stretching exercises can be done seven days a week. They should be done at least three days a week to keep yourself limber. Almost everyone has back pain at some time in their lives. I never have had back pains that lasted more than 24 hours and I attribute it to the fact that I have done these stretching exercises religiously for twenty-five years.

The last time I can recall having any back pain at all was when I was driving across country. About five days out, my back started to hurt and I realized that I hadn't been doing my exercises. That night I did a few stretches, and the next morning, before going to breakfast, I did the complete set of stretching exercises. By the time I got into the car that morning, the pain was gone.

A twenty-minute brisk walk every day, or even three or four days a week, will help elevate your mood, your metabolism and your energy level. Even if you play tennis, racquetball or golf or ride a bicycle, it is still important to get out and just walk regularly. This is a time for you to clear your mind and repeat your affirmations to yourself. The visualizations you do when you relax can also be done as you walk.

Choose a time according to your own circadian rhythm to exercise and then do it faithfully at the same time every day. As there are cycles of light and darkness as our planet spins on its axis every twenty-four hours, we have basic planetary rhythms built into our systems. There are daily fluctuations in the release of neurotransmitters in our brains and nervous systems as well as in the biochemistry of all our cells. Our sleep patterns, fertile periods and energy levels all seem to be related to these diurnal changes.

For some people, morning is the best time to exercise; for others it may be late afternoon or evening. You will probably get the most benefit from your exercise if you do it when your energy level is at its highest. If morning is best for you, get up a half-hour earlier and exercise right before breakfast or your morning shower. If it's at noon, you can take a light lunch to work and take half of your lunch hour to walk. Or you might find the most comfortable plan for you is to do your stretching exercises in the morning and to take your walk in the evening before dinner. Whichever you decide, keep to a regular schedule. It will soon become a pattern.

If you change nothing else in your life, you will notice a difference if you make exercise a habit. You will burn hundreds of extra calories a week and your metabolism will speed up. Even if you do not cut down on the calories you consume, you will lose weight. Within a month you can easily lose five pounds.

When you exercise you are forced to breathe more deeply. Your lung capacity will increase and your lungs will clean out much sooner than they would if you did not exercise.

Not only your physical energy but your mental energy will improve. Your memory will get sharper and you will find a renewed enthusiasm for learning. You will probably sleep less but sleep more soundly.

Walking is one of the best, if not the best, exercise you can do for total body benefit. Swimming is also good because it exercises most of the muscles in your body. But for women it may not be as good as walking because it is not a weight-bearing exercise, so it won't help as much as walking in the prevention of osteoporosis.

Chapter 10

*Putting It All Together—
Ten Easy Steps*

Up to now you have learned about the difference between the female addiction to smoking and the male addiction. You now have a better idea of why women usually started smoking as young teenagers and why it is so hard for them to quit. You are getting in touch with *yourself* and understanding some of the reasons *you* still smoke in spite of all the dire statistics about women and smoking. You have all the facts you need to help you decide whether to quit smoking. You know that it is something you must do to protect your health and to prolong your life and, perhaps, even to save it.

I hope that you are now convinced not only that you must quit smoking but that you *can* quit smoking. And you are determined to do so!

The decision to quit smoking for good and the determination to follow through on that decision is the most important factor in overcoming your addiction. Without that firm resolve, quitting will be difficult, painful and, probably, even impossible.

Ten Easy Steps

Once you have made the decision, following these ten easy steps will make your journey from smoker to nonsmoker more comfortable, productive and rewarding. They have all been addressed in detail in previous chapters. Now it's time to start putting them all together and mapping out a master plan for yourself.

1. Make out a weekly schedule.

Decide at what time each day you will practice your deep breathing, relaxation and visualization. Plan your day around these and your exercise schedule.

Figure 2 gives you an example of a weekly schedule. On Monday, the imaginary woman in this plan does her deep breathing, relaxation and visualization exercises when she first wakes up in the morning. (Deep breathing always precedes the relaxation and visualization exercises.) She may take 20 minutes to do the exercise, 10 minutes to dress and then stretches and walks for the next 30 to 45 minutes. She has breakfast and prepares her snacks for the day. She does the deep breathing for a couple of minutes, at least three times throughout the day. At bedtime, just before she goes to sleep, she does the deep breathing, relaxation and visualization exercise again.

If this is her PMS week, she will carefully plan what she will eat this week. She may make notes at the bottom of the page to remind herself to shop for and/or eat foods on her PMS list this week. If she takes a ten-minute break twice a day at her job and usually

Figure 2

Stop Smoking Schedule - Week of _____

Time		Sun	Mon	Tues	Wed	Thurs	Fri	Sat
1								
2								
3								
4	A.M.							
5	5:45		Relax/visualize	Relax/visualize		Relax/visualize	Relax/visualize	
6	6:15		Stretch, walk	Bicycle	Relax/visualize	Bicycle	Stretch, walk	
7	7:00		Breakfast	Breakfast	Breakfast mtg.	Breakfast	Breakfast	Relax/visualize
8	8:00				Stretch			Breakfast
9	9:00		Deep breathe	Deep breathe	Deep breathe	Deep breathe	Deep breathe	Tennis lesson
10	10:00		Snack	Snack	Snack	Snack	Snack	Snack
11	11:00							Play tennis
12	NOON		Lunch	Lunch	Lunch/walk	Lunch	Lunch	
13	1:00							Lunch
14	2:00		Deep breathe	Deep breathe	Deep breathe	Deep breathe	Deep breathe	Deep breathe
15	3:00		Snack	Snack	Snack	Snack	Snack	Jewelry project
16	4:00							Snack
17	5:00		Deep breathe	Deep breathe	Deep breathe	Deep breathe	Deep breathe	Deep breathe
18	6:00		Dinner	Dinner	Run errands	Dinner	Dinner	
19	7:00			Jewelry class	Dinner w/ Mom	Smokers Anon.		Deep breathe
20	8:00							Dinner out
21	9:00							Concert
22	10:00		Relax/visualize	Relaz/visualize	Relax/visualize	Relax/visualize	Relax/visualize	
23	11:00							
24	12 M							Relax/visualize

Chapter 10

147

smoked a cigarette or two during this time, she will do her deep breathing and have her snack instead.

Although the example shows a very structured schedule, you will note that it allows for variables. For instance, on Wednesday, this woman sleeps in later than usual and has a breakfast meeting. She does her stretching exercises right after breakfast and fits in her walking during her lunch hour.

At least once a week, it's a good idea to get involved in a group of people who are overcoming their addiction to smoking, too. An excellent one is Smokers Anonymous, a 12-step program. The woman in our example has put it in her schedule every Thursday evening. If there is not one in your area, you may be able to start one.

Her Saturday schedule differs from her workday schedule, but she plans that day, too, making sure she has time for playing and for her hobbies. You will notice in this schedule that Sunday is blank. That is because Sundays may be completely unstructured unless you find them a problem for you. If you do, plan that day, too.

figure 3 is a blank schedule that you may use to devise your own plan. You may want to write in the actual time frame in which you intend to do each thing; for instance, "stretching and walking: 7:00 to 7:30." You may not follow this schedule exactly every day but you will have guidelines to aim for.

If you are not planning to quit cold, you may want to put into the schedule the number of cigarettes you will allow yourself to smoke each day and at what times you will smoke them. You may decide to quit entirely

Figure 3

Stop Smoking Schedule - Week of _____

Time	Sun	Mon	Tues	Wed	Thurs	Fri	Sat
1							
2							
3							
4 A.M.							
5 5:45							
6 6:15							
7 7:00							
8 8:00							
9 9:00							
10 10:00							
11 11:00							
12 NOON							
13 1:00							
14 2:00							
15 3:00							
16 4:00							
17 5:00							
18 6:00							
19 7:00							
20 8:00							
21 9:00							
22 10:00							
23 11:00							
24 12 M							

Chapter 10

over a period of three to six weeks and to reduce the number of cigarettes you smoke each week as outlined in Chapter Three. In that case, make notes at the bottom of each weekly schedule outlining your plan to cut down and indicating the number of cigarettes you will be limiting yourself to that week.

2. Practice deep breathing

Do your deep-breathing exercise several times a day and before each relaxation and visualization exercise. Whenever you feel nervous or have urges for a cigarette, take several deep breaths. It will help you calm yourself down and "wait out" those urges. As you breathe deeply, focus on how good your lungs feel breathing in clean, fresh, smoke-free air.

Concentrate on your breathing and stay in the moment. Don't let your mind drift into thinking about failures in the past or worries about the future. (See Chapter Eight)

3. Relax and visualize a healthier, happier you

Twice a day practice relaxing your body and mind completely and visualizing yourself in a beautiful place. Imagine yourself healthier than you've ever been, breathing clear air into your healthy lungs, feeling a greater sense of freedom and vitality. These sessions optimally should be in the morning when you first awaken to prepare you for the day and the last thing you do at night before sleeping to help program your subconscious mind.

Make your own relaxation tape, using your own

voice and verbally describing your favorite place and how you feel. (See chapter Eight)

4. *Exercise. Stretch and walk daily.*

Whether or not you play any sports, it is important to stretch every morning to keep yourself limber. You should walk at least three times a week and preferably five. Ten minutes of stretching and twenty minutes of walking are very beneficial. If you can find the time to walk a hour a day, it's even better. While you are walking, practice your visualizations and affirmations. Tell yourself how healthy, happy, intelligent, calm, loving, etc. you are. This is a good time to start building more self-esteem. (See Chapter Nine)

5. *Plan your meals and snacks*

Copy the foods on the list that you should eat during that week or two before your period when you may experience premenstrual tension. Make a grocery list that includes those foods so that you may keep them in the house at all times. If you eat out more often than you eat at home, take your list with you and check it before you order. In most places you can find things on the menu that will fill the requirements. Eat fresh foods including raw fruits and vegetables as often as you can. Limit intake of red meats and increase whole grains, nuts and beans. Avoid fast food places.

Eat five or six times a day instead of only three. Prepare snacks to take with you each day so that you don't experience hunger pains. (See Chapters Two and Nine)

6. *Replace the urges with more positive thoughts*

Associate smoking with something negative. Recall how bad your car, your house, your clothing and even your breath smelled. When you have the urge for a cigarette, immediately change your thoughts to something you enjoy. Think of your favorite place, take a deep breath and thank yourself for how healthy you feel now that you are no longer smoking. Imagine a smile on the face of someone you love. (See Chapters Six and Seven)

7. *Get a hobby, keep your hands busy with arts and crafts*

That old adage "Idle hands are the devil's tools" is never more true than when you apply it to smoking. Your hands have gotten used to lighting that cigarette, putting it to your mouth, taking a puff and pulling the smoke into your lungs. There has been a ritual around using your cigarette lighter, tapping off the ashes, watching the smoke curl and rise in the air, even to snubbing your cigarette out in an ashtray or grinding it into the ground with your foot. Many people miss that ritual. It must be replaced with some other ritual. Finding a hobby that uses your hands is the best way to keep your hands and mind occupied and off cigarettes.

Take classes, join a photography club, knit, crochet, paint, sculpt, make jewelry or furniture. Get involved in some productive hobby and create a ritual around it. You will actually have more time now that you are not smoking. Not only does the act of smoking take up a certain amount of time but you probably had to go outside to smoke and you wasted a lot of time just standing and puffing.

8. *Give yourself a treat each day*

Buy yourself a bouquet of flowers. Take a long, luxurious bubble bath. Put your favorite perfume on the back of your hand and sniff it whenever you resist the urge for a cigarette.

Buy yourself a present with the money you save by not buying cigarettes. Take yourself and a friend or lover out to dinner in a fine restaurant. Prepare a gourmet meal, pour yourself a glass of your favorite wine (or other beverage), put on some beautiful music and dine by candlelight.

Get a manicure, a pedicure or both. Get new designer sheets. Buy a new pair of shoes. Get a new haircut, color your hair or get a perm. It's a new you. Enjoy yourself.

9. *Get in touch with your feelings, build self-esteem*

Appreciate and try to understand your feelings. Feelings are neither right nor wrong but they can be negative or positive and you will want to practice having more positive feelings than negative ones. Look for the good in people and in situations. Refuse to feel self-pity. You are not giving up an old friend when you quit smoking. You are giving yourself a new and wonderful gift.

Make sure you notice how much better you are feeling and looking now. Allow yourself to feel the joy of your rediscovered inner strength. Let yourself acknowledge your successes and be proud of yourself. Make a list of all the things you have done that have been successful. Make another list of all of your attributes, strengths and talents. Refer to these lists often.

10. Love yourself and thank your higher power
You did it! You made the decision and you made the commitment to quit smoking. By now, you may have actually quit. And you never could have if you didn't love yourself. You couldn't have done it without the help of someone or something greater than yourself. Whether you call this power God or a higher consciousness, your own spirit or simply your own dogged determination, you found within yourself the power to take control of your own life and overcome an incredibly powerful addiction.

If you have not actually snuffed out your last cigarette by now, then this is the time to do it. Right now. Today. You have all the tools. Believe you can do it and you can.

Chapter 11

Reinforce Your Resolve

Now that you've quit smoking will you ever have the urge for a cigarette again? For most people, the answer is yes, most likely you will. In this chapter you will learn coping strategies. You will learn a number of things that you can do to help you remain a nonsmoker.

When do those urges happen? Is it after dinner, with a drink, after sex, while you are driving? Make a list of the times that the urges are the strongest. Write down all that you can think of, then give them a number from one to ten as to their intensity. For instance, if the cigarette you want the most all day is the one after dinner, give that one a 10. If it's hard to decide which is the most intense, you can assign a 10 to several of the incidents in which you have the urge to smoke. Here is a list of some of the triggers. If all of yours aren't on this list, add them to it.

    ___ When I first get up in the morning
    ___ With my first cup of coffee
    ___ After breakfast
    ___ When I get in the car and turn on the ignition
    ___ Waiting for a bus, subway or plane
    ___ On my work break

___ After lunch
___ While cooking dinner
___ After dinner
___ After sex
___ With coffee, tea, soft drink
___ Getting ready for work
___ When I first get home from work
___ When I am hungry
___ Watching television
___ At a sports event
___ Whenever I have a conflict with my husband, lover, children, boss
___ When I am at a party
___ When I finish a chore

___ _____
___ _____
___ _____
___ _____
___ _____

Being aware of the situations that trigger strong urges to smoke helps you prepare for them. As each situation is different, what you do in each one will be different. Except for two things. In each case, the first thing to do is take a few deep breaths. This helps you relax and wait out the urge until it fades away. If you have found the beach pebble or some other small object helpful, then place that in the palm of your hand and note how long it takes to warm to the temperature of your hand. By the time it is warm, the greatest intensity of your urge will have passed.

Find the way to handle each specific situation that works best for you. The following are some suggestions:

As mentioned earlier, if you have a strong desire for a cigarette on your work break, you may want to snack on carrot or celery sticks and take a walk.

If the urge is strongest when you first awake, keep a cinnamon stick and a glass of water by your bed. Take a big drink and put the cinnamon stick in your mouth. If it is after breakfast, get up immediately from the table and brush your teeth.

Take something with you to read while waiting for a bus, subway, train or plane. Or take along your knitting or crocheting. Take a sketch pad and sketch the scene or the people. Take a small notebook and make notes of your observations. Any of these will help you take your mind off your urges and keep your hands busy.

If your favorite cigarette of the day was after dinner, then immediately get up from the table and do the dishes, take a walk, work on your hobby or take a shower. Create new habits for those difficult times.

If you most want a cigarette with your first cup of coffee of the day, switch to tea or a glass of juice.

Instead of lighting a cigarette after making love, try holding your mate and telling him all the things you love about him. You may start a conversation that will open up a whole new wonderful way of relating to each other.

Does the ring of the phone make you salivate for a cigarette? Keep a large pad of paper and colored marking pens by the telephone. When it rings, pick up the pens and start to draw or just doodle.

Keep barbells by your desk and when you have the urge to slip out of the office for a cigarette, pick them up and do arm lifts for a few minutes. This will help you firm up your upper arms and make you stronger. You may even develop some biceps and that's okay. That's considered quite attractive in women today. There are also gadgets to exercise your hands with. They are especially helpful if you are at a computer for several hours every day. They will help strengthen your hands, avoid carpel tunnel syndrome and give your hands an excellent substitute for a cigarette.

Had a bad day at work? When you come home, fix yourself a nice, hot cup of herb tea and write about it in your journal. By the way, there is probably a journal writing group or class in your area that you could join. Writing in your journal not only keeps your hands busy but it keeps your mind busy working on the challenges in your life. It helps you get in touch with your feelings, which is essential in breaking any habit or addiction.

Get yourself a guitar and take guitar lessons. Once you've got a few chords down you can begin to accompany yourself as you sing. Even if you don't play guitar, sing around the house. Not even Sinatra could sing and smoke at the same time. Or get some music on the radio and dance.

Be good to yourself. Draw yourself a deep, hot bath, put pungent herbal salts in it, light some candles, put on a record of Gregorian chants and soak in the tub until you are relaxed bone-deep.

Feeling lonely? Call a friend and go out to a movie. Or rent a movie, pop some popcorn and invite someone over for the evening. Write a long letter to someone dear to you.

Prepare for contingencies

The important thing is to plan for these times and prepare for contingencies. What are you going to do if you suddenly get called into the boss's office, or you have a fight with a loved one, or you narrowly avoid having an accident (or do have an accident), or your car breaks down, or your child gets into trouble at school? You aren't going to handle stressful situations by lighting up anymore, so how will you handle them?

After taking several deep breaths, visualize your special place where you feel peaceful and calm and remember your promise to yourself—that nothing is going to stand in the way of your good health. Without delay, handle the situation. Immediately take action. Tell yourself that whatever it is, you are in control of your feelings. Ask your higher power, your subconscious mind, or wherever you believe your inner strength resides, for guidance.

Let everyone know that you have quit smoking and ask them for help. If they know that you are irritable because you are changing your way of life and breaking an addiction, they may find it easier to be patient with you.

Avoid being with smokers if at all possible for the first few weeks. It may make it harder to remain a nonsmoker if you are around people who are smoking. However, this is not always the case. I know of several people to whom that made no difference at all. One of my clients carpooled with three other people who all smoked. She didn't start driving to work alone, nor did she ask them not to smoke when she was in the car. She was so determined not to smoke that she just decided it wasn't going to bother her and it didn't.

When I stopped smoking I was married to a smoker who didn't stop when I did. He was very understanding, though, because he knew I had an immediate medical reason to quit. Several times I asked him—no, *begged him*, for a cigarette and he refused to give me one. After a few days I quit asking. I found that it helped me, though, to empty and wash his ashtray every time he put a cigarette out. If I hadn't I was afraid that I'd smoke one of the butts.

I never nagged him not to smoke because I knew it wouldn't help. I remembered how stubborn I would get when someone nagged me. Within a couple of months he quit smoking, too. He said he was tired of having to dirty a clean ashtray with each cigarette.

No one knows what will work with a specific person. Something inside us has to decide once and for all that we are no longer going to smoke. Then we each have to find the strength within ourselves to maintain our resolve never to smoke again. We have to replace the cigarette with something better.

For most people who have been successful in quitting smoking for good there was an awakening, a sudden knowing, an inexplicable feeling that they would let nothing stand in their way of success. It was an unshakable determination to take control of their lives. This turning point can be reached by anyone. The path you take will be your own personal path and only you can find it. But when you do, that path leads to freedom and a new, healthier and happier life. And it's so worth it!

Keep in touch with yourself
You are starting a new lifestyle and must get rid of old triggers, messages and ways of doing things. Now is the time to break old habit patterns, to stop doing routine things each day automatically. You must learn to be in touch with your thinking and your feelings at all times, to stay in the present and not let your mind drift off into old, familiar worries and insecurities.

There are several ways of changing habits. Start first thing in the morning by putting your shoes on differently. If you always put your left shoe on first, shift to putting on your right shoe first.

Drive a different route to work or any place you go to often. Find as many different routes as you can and vary them each day. That way, you won't just put your mind on automatic pilot. You will be more aware the whole time you are driving.

Make sure you have breakfast every morning. But not the same old thing every day. Have toast one morning, cereal the next and now and then go out for a nice, big breakfast.

Do a little housecleaning each evening during the week so your weekend is free to do something really different. Join the Sierra Club or the Audubon Society and go on hikes. Walk precincts or hand out flyers for your favorite politician or cause.

Start reading a book at least part of every evening instead of watching TV. Take a class or work on a project in the evening.

Send personal notes or greeting cards to friends and family on special occasions in their lives. This helps you take your mind off yourself and will surprise and please those you love.

Start a journal and write in it every day. Make notes of your feelings, observations, progress, anything that is of interest to you.

Find new interests and pursue them. Go to concerts in the park, to a cat show or to a film festival. Visit a local museum or art gallery.

Give a surprise birthday party for a friend. Look up someone who was special to you in the past, like a high school teacher or an old friend you've lost touch with and give them a call or write to them telling them how much they meant to you.

Take some stuffed toys to children in the hospital. Or just visit them and read them stories.

There are so many wonderful things to do in this world, not only for yourself but for others. When you think about others and do things for them, you not only take your mind off your own troubles, you make their lives better, too, and that can bring you a great deal of personal joy and self-esteem.

An important part of breaking any addiction or healing any illness or pain is finding a new, different and better way to spend your time and to live your life.

Practice your own "fire drill"

Write out the ways you are going to handle "slippery situations," those times when the urge for a cigarette seems overpowering. What are you going to do when you have an argument with a loved one? How are you going to handle an upset at work? What are you going to do with your hands at a party? By projecting what could happen in the future that could trigger the desire to smoke, you can plan your counterattack and visualize yourself carrying it out.

Studies have shown that people who practiced fire drills were more likely to be able to save themselves in a fire. They knew where the exits were. They had a plan and they didn't panic. They simply did what they had been trained to do.

You can do this, too. Right now, write down every situation you can think of that may present a challenge to your remaining a nonsmoker and how you are going to handle it. Then read it over again at least once a day and visualize yourself being successful in dealing with every possible challenge.

Write down your list of challenges and how you plan to face them here:

_____
_____
_____
_____
_____
_____
_____
_____
_____
_____
_____

Chapter 12

Now You're Really Living

There is no magic pill you can take that will keep you from ever wanting to smoke again. As mentioned before, the nicotine patch has been a great disappointment to many smokers who have used it. And all it does really is deliver nicotine to your system in a different way. I don't believe that the nicotine addiction can be overcome by merely changing the delivery system. If someone can be addicted to cigarettes, couldn't they also become addicted to nicotine gum or the nicotine patch? It is the nicotine that is addictive, not any other property of the cigarette.

There is no question that nicotine is a powerful pharmacological agent. Not only does it affect heart rate and blood pressure but it alters other important body functions. It alters brain function and affects the users mood, feelings and behavior. Like other addictive drugs, these changes can lead to corresponding adaptations in nervous system function. Eventually, the brain and nervous system begin to require nicotine just to function normally. It is these factors that define nicotine as an addictive drug.

As many as 90 percent of all smokers are

physically addicted to nicotine, according to the 1988 Surgeon General's report, *The Health Consequences of Smoking: Nicotine Addiction.* In testimony before the House Energy and Commerce Committee, it was brought out that this is higher than the proportion of *cocaine and heroin users who are addicted to those substances.*

There is a striking relationship between tobacco use and other substance-abuse problems. In one study the criterion for alcohol abuse was the consumption of five or more drinks in a row on at least one day in the past 30 days. The criteria for marijuana and cocaine were to have used them more than ten times *ever*. Survey data showing that only about 10 percent of smokers smoke five cigarettes or less a day is strong evidence that tobacco use is a compulsive behavior. As at least two-thirds of smokers have tried unsuccessfully to quit, it is clear that tobacco has taken control of their behaviors.

According to the 1989 Surgeon General's Report, *Reducing the Health Consequences of Smoking: 25 Years of Progress,* the hallmark of drug dependence disorders or diseases is the highly controlled or compulsive use of a substance that contains a psychoactive chemical. The terms *drug addiction* or *drug dependence* apply as much to cigarette smokers as they do to users of any other drugs including heroin and cocaine.

A 1990 report of the *Journal of General Internal Medicine* states that compulsive use of a drug can take control over behavior in two ways: by its direct rewarding effects or by unpleasant withdrawal symptoms. Nicotine does both. It has been shown to cause changes in electroencephalogram (EEG) activity. It can alter both mood and feeling states, much as other addictive drugs do. Nicotine can alleviate anxiety and boredom as do many narcotics. Nicotine deprivation causes a dysphoric state and behavioral deficits. It is not yet clear to most researchers whether the rewarding properties of nicotine come from direct positive effects of the drug or from the relief of withdrawal symptoms.

The above facts are presented to give you a clear picture of what smoking is really all about. If you are a smoker, you are probably addicted and your addiction is not very different from that of the users of "hard drugs." In fact, the major difference is that tobacco is a legal drug.

With more and more stringent laws being enacted about nicotine use, it will become harder to find places to buy cigarettes, they will become more expensive and there will be even fewer places where they can be smoked. If ever there was a time to quit smoking, *this is it!*

Withdrawal symptoms

If you ever tried to quit smoking before, you were probably aware of some of the following withdrawal symptoms: craving, irritability, difficulty in concentrating, anxiety, restlessness and increased appetite. You may have had headaches, felt light-headed or had difficulty in sleeping.

You may not have to experience any of these if you follow the suggestions in this book. By now, you will know whether the gradual or the cold turkey approach is best for you.

Whichever way you quit smoking you can relieve or eliminate withdrawal symptoms by making sure that you eat the appropriate foods for different phases of your monthly cycle. Exercise and changing your routines will help break some of the automatic responses to triggers. Regularly practicing deep breathing will relieve stress and smoking urges. Relaxation and visualization exercises will help you to "reset" your subconscious mind and aim it toward a more healthful lifestyle.

It's important to remember that even if you do have withdrawal feelings, they do not last very long, and the rewards of quitting smoking more than make up for any temporary discomfort.

The good news is that over 38 million Americans have quit smoking, according to the 1990 Surgeon General's Report. The *Journal of the American Medical Association*, May 23/30, 1990 issue, states that each year about 1.3 million smokers quit successfully. If they can do it, you can do it too.

Identify the stressors in your life and deal with them

In order to break the nicotine addiction, what we need to do is change ourselves. The major reason people smoke is to relieve stress. Smoking helps them to distance themselves from their troubles. Many people use alcohol in the same way, to escape and avoid dealing with their problems. But problems and stressors don't just magically go away with a drink or a smoke. They are only covered up and tuned out. They are only delayed.

The only way to truly get rid of the stress in our lives is to find out what is causing it and then deal with it. We can't get past our problems and relieve the stress they cause us unless we face them. In the same way, we can't get rid of our urges to smoke until we find the triggers and disarm them.

Expand your horizons

Once you regain control of yourself in regard to your smoking, you should feel a new sense of freedom and power. If you can overcome your addiction to nicotine, you can do just about anything. You have already embarked on a journey toward a more healthy lifestyle. Now is the time to expand your horizons and be everything you can be.

To continue on your path of learning, of self-discovery and healing, there are a number of things you can do. To start with, you must learn to live in the present. After all, the past is gone forever. We can't go back and change a thing no matter how much we may want to. It's fruitless to think and worry about what might have been. We can't have been a better mother, we can only be a better mother from now on. We can't have taken a different path, made different decisions, taken a different job, gotten out of a bad relationship sooner. We did what seemed to be the right thing at the time or what we thought was our only choice.

Live in the present

Just as we cannot change the past, we can't live in the future. The future is only a dream and cannot be known. If we live our lives thinking that we'll be happy in some mythical tomorrow when we will have finished our education, gotten married, gotten a promotion or the car or the house or the children we've always wanted, we will be living for the future.

We may think that if we only had a lot of money or true love we'd be happy. But as long as we let our happiness depend on something we hope to attain someday in some other place or time, we will be postponing our very lives.

When I was a child I read a story called, "The Bluebird of Happiness." All I can recall of the story was that it was about a person who searched the world over for the Bluebird of Happiness and never found it. When she finally gave up and came home, she looked out of her window and saw it in her own back yard. And it had been there all along.

Make your own happiness

We think we can find happiness somewhere else, with someone else, at some other time or when some certain thing happens. But when we reach that "somewhere" and we're with that "someone" and all is not perfect, we start looking for some other person or future event as being that which will make us happy at last. And so it goes.

All we truly have is this moment. This is where we live now. Or, maybe a better way of saying it is *now is where we live.* And if we are to find happiness we must find it here and now. We must learn to live in the moment. Living in the moment is not the same as living *for* the moment. Living in the moment doesn't mean never planning for the future. It simply means keeping ourselves in the present.

We still must get an education, work on our relationships, save our money and take care of our health. It is certainly important to prepare ourselves for a long life and to do what is necessary to help assure that our future will be bright. But we can do all of these while we are living in the present, enjoying the people we are with and the things we are doing.

The mind/body connection

There is a new branch of medicine known as behavioral medicine or mind/body medicine which operates on the belief that mental and emotional factors play a major role, for better or worse, in our physical health and our capacity to heal. In major medical centers there are now stress reduction programs. And what most of them teach is the art of conscious living.

Nowhere is this more beneficial than in the treatment of addictions. Smoking, as well as other addictions, affect and are affected by our mental, psychological and physical health. It is true that if you stop smoking you will most likely be healthier. It's also true that when you become healthier you will find it easier to stop smoking. Especially when you become emotionally healthier.

By learning to have moment-to-moment

awareness we can develop more control and greater wisdom in our lives. It does take effort and determination on our part, but by mobilizing our own inner capacity for growth and healing we can take charge of our lives.

Develop your awareness through your five senses

There is an exercise to help you develop your awareness by getting in touch with all of your senses. By practicing this often, you might even find that you are able to develop what some call a "sixth sense." There may or may not truly be such a thing, but by becoming acutely aware at all times of all of the recognized senses that we do have, we can greatly heighten our five senses. We can become so completely tuned in to ourselves and our surroundings that we may actually develop what would seem to be extrasensory perception or "ESP."

The following is an exercise designed to help you get in touch with your senses. As you do each one, concentrate on that alone and ignore any other sensory input. If your thoughts wander off, bring them back to the moment and what you sensing. Focus on each sense as intensely as possible and to the exclusion of all others.

Find a quiet, comfortable and peaceful place where you can either be alone or can disappear into the scenery. This preferably would be outdoors. It might be in the woods, at the beach, in the desert or in the mountains, but it should be someplace which is not crowded or noisy.

This is a walking exercise, so be sure that you have on loose clothing and comfortable shoes and that you are not carrying anything. Walk at an easy, natural pace, neither rushing nor unusually slow.

The sense of taste:

Starting with the sense of taste, notice whether you can taste anything. It might be the taste of your toothpaste or some food you ate recently whose flavor lingers in your mouth. Being careful not to get any poisonous plant, break off a leaf, blade of grass or blossom and place a small particle of it in your mouth. Notice the flavor. If you are at the beach, dip your finger into the water, touch it to your tongue and taste the salt. Now, think of all of your favorite foods and try to imagine the sweetness or saltiness of them. Let yourself remember the taste of the seasonings and all of the different flavors that are contained in each one. Make a mental note to eat your next meal very slowly and notice the taste of every item. Try to pick out individual flavors in each one: the garlic or cheese in pasta or pizza; the vanilla flavoring in your ice cream; the herbs in your salad dressing, etc.

The sense of touch:

As you walk, feel the ground beneath your feet. Is it soft? Is it hard? Feel your toes and notice how they help to keep you balanced. Feel the air on your face. Is it warm? Cool? Feel the sun on your body. Feel your clothing touching your body, moving and brushing against your skin slightly with each step. Feel your hair ruffling gently in the breeze. Stroke your arm lightly from your shoulder to the tips of your fingers and feel how your hand feels as it touches you through your clothing or on your bare skin. Run your fingers through your hair. Sit down now and touch the different textures around you: the sand, the dirt, the pebbles, the decaying leaves, the flowers, moss or bark of a tree. Close your eyes as you touch them and let yourself imagine that you are actually seeing them through your fingertips. If there is water around, put your hand in it, move it slowly back and forth and feel the soft and slippery feeling of the water encircling your hand. Notice the temperature of the water. Then take your hand out of the water and notice how it feels as it dries. Concentrate on your breathing and feel the air going in and out of your body. Breathing deeply, feel your lungs expand as they fill with air.

The sense of smell:

Take a handful of dirt or sand or crumbled, dried leaves and put it under your nose. What do you smell? Is there very little odor or is it pungent? As you rise, do you notice a difference in the scent of the air? Do you smell pine trees, eucalyptus, honeysuckle, sagebrush, wild fennel, smoke, new-mown grass, food cooking? Try to identify all of the scents. As you walk, break off pieces of leaves from the surrounding vegetation, crush them in your fingers and sniff them. Are they wild herbs? Do any of them smell like nothing you have ever smelled before? Can you smell the odors on your own body? Your perfume? Your shampoo?

Your lotion? Your own body aroma? We each have our own body smell—not good or bad—but just a scent that is uniquely ours. If you are in the woods or at the beach, can you detect the scent of wildlife or sea animals?

The sense of hearing:

Listen. What do you hear? Can you hear the traffic? Can you discern whether they are trucks or cars? Can you hear a train? Are there voices within your range of hearing? Are they laughing, yelling, speaking softly? Are they excited or calm? Do you hear dogs barking, cats meowing, birds singing? Can you hear more than one bird song? Can you hear the wind in the trees? Is there a hum of a motor anywhere near? Can you hear the waves lapping against the shore? If you can hear footsteps, is the person walking or running? Can you guess the age and sex of the person by their footsteps? Can you hear a small animal like a rabbit, a squirrel or a lizard darting about among the leaves on the ground? Can you hear a cat climbing a tree? Listen to all the sounds and try to distinguish them from one another. Identify as many different sounds as you can.

The sense of sight:

First of all, notice the time of day. Is it morning, afternoon or evening? Which way do the shadows fall? Is it bright and sunny or overcast? Are there clouds in the sky? Birds? Insects? An airplane or helicopter? How many different kinds of trees do you see? Is anything in bloom? Are there people around? How old are they?

What are they doing? How are they dressed? Do you see any animals? Are they small or large, friendly or aloof, male or female? If there are buildings in sight, are they residences or businesses? How many stories do they have? If you are in the woods or desert, what kinds of plants grow close to the ground? Look very closely at them. Are there tiny flowers on them? What color are they and how many petals do they have? If you are at the beach, can you see any shells, shiny pebbles or pieces of glass, cloudy and smoothed by tumbling in the sea? Look all around you, up and down. How many colors can you see? What is the predominant color? Gray or brown? Blue (sky)? Green (plants)? Observe the color of everything you see and notice the various shadings in each one. Look, *really look*, at things you may never have noticed before. Notice all of the minute details of each object your eyes fall on.

Now, stop, sit down and get comfortable. Let all of the parts of your awareness come together, keenly sensing everything that is going on around you. Let your *full Self* feel. Turn your observations inward and feel your heart beat, imagine your blood coursing through your veins, experience your breathing. Sense your nails and hair growing and your skin shedding its outer layer and renewing itself from within. Observe the amazing machine that is your body. Notice how efficiently it takes care of everything without any instructions from you. All you need to do is feed it, exercise it, keep it warm, show it love.

Now, take your mind off of everything and just *be*. This is what it means to live *in the moment*.

If you have lost or if you never had any one of the five senses, you probably have developed one or more of the other senses to a high degree. Those who are born blind develop a keen sense of touch and hearing. Deaf people are more aware of vibrations and other sensory stimuli. Much can be learned from these people whom society once called "handicapped." They are probably the true experts on developing the senses to their highest possible plane.

Once you learn to get in touch with your *Self*, you will be aware every time you are not good to yourself. Once you are able to truly appreciate and love your body with all its incredible senses, you will not want to do anything to harm it. You will become keenly aware of the air you breathe and how it feels entering and leaving your body. If you smoke or breathe other people's smoke, you will be aware of how that smoke feels in your mouth and in your throat. You mind will trace it as it travels down your windpipe and into your lungs. You will feel its heat and sense its toxicity. You will be so aware that you will never smoke a cigarette again *automatically*. You will be aware of each and every puff.

When you reach that point, it will simply be a matter of deciding, consciously, whether or not you will continue to smoke. You will be in charge again.

Remember always that your life is in your hands. No matter what happened to you in the past, you are in charge of yourself now. You may not have complete control over everything that will happen in the future but you can determine how it will affect you. You can decide how to act and react in many different situations. You can lead a happier, healthier life. Not only can you quit smoking forever, you can decide to start now to change your entire life for the better.

Look on this day as being the most important day of your life. And look on this moment as the only time that matters. Because it is.

A MESSAGE FROM THE PUBLISHER

I have been amazed that since the Surgeon General's Report of 1964 there have been so few stop-smoking programs addressed to the special needs of women. Women do, indeed, require a different approach to stopping smoking, and Mary Embree, a former smoker herself who has lost loved ones to smoking, addresses those unique needs with this excellent guide toward wholeness and healing from the addiction of smoking. I wholeheartedly recommend it to you if you are a smoker and/or as a gift to a female loved one who has been unsuccessful in her battle with addiction.

W. R. Spence, M.D.
Publisher

At WRS Publishing, we are only interested in producing books that we can be proud of—books that focus on people and/or issues that enlighten and inspire, books that change lives for the better. Call us toll-free at 1-800-299-3366 for suggestions or for a free book catalog.

WATCH FOR THESE OTHER WRS TITLES:

LIFE ISN'T WEIGHED ON THE BATHROOM SCALES Laura Rose empowers the reader to reverse two basic lies taught to most of us: **First,** that you can lose weight *easily* if you want it badly enough, and **second**, that you can't fulfill your potential until you get thin. Rose's life and her own research affirm that fat people are not only physically healthy, but emotionally, mentally, and spiritually healthy as well.

IN TOUCH WITH YOUR BREASTS provides the answers to women's questions about breastcare. Written by a surgeon who specializes in breast problems, this book addresses all diseases and conditions of the breast in an easy-to-understand question-and-answer format and it includes a lifelike miniature breast to teach breast self-examination.

THE ART OF STEPMOTHERING Stories about and solutions to the problems and anxieties of stepmothering from Pearl Prilik, herself a stepmother. A down-to-earth guide for dealing with real-life situations.

WRS PUBLISHING
A Division of WRS Group, Inc.
Waco, Texas